westermann

Pathway
Approach

Prep & Practice Book

Herausgegeben und erarbeitet von
Iris Edelbrock

Sprachliche Betreuung
Dr. Michelle Ruth Büscher

Pathway
Approach

Zusatzmaterialien zu Pathway Approach
Für Lehrerinnen und Lehrer:

Teachers' Manual	978-3-14-121503-8
BiBox Einzellizenz für Lehrer/-innen (Dauerlizenz)	WEB-14-121509
BiBox Kollegiumslizenz für Lehrer/-innen (Dauerlizenz)	WEB-14-121510
BiBox Kollegiumslizenz für Lehrer/-innen (1 Schuljahr)	WEB-14-107424

Mehr Informationen über aktuelle Lizenzen finden Sie auf www.bibox.schule.

Für Schülerinnen und Schüler:

BiBox Einzellizenz für Schüler/-innen (1 Schuljahr)	WEB-14-121506

westermann GRUPPE

Druck A[1] / Jahr 2022
Alle Drucke der Serie A sind im Unterricht parallel verwendbar.

Redaktion: Marion Kramer, Anna-Marina Vogt
Sprachliche Betreuung und Lösungen: Dr. Michelle Ruth Büscher
Umschlaggestaltung: LIO Design, Foto: Mark Gibson/Alamy Stock Photo
Layout: Alexandra Brand, Paderborn
Druck und Bindung: Westermann Druck GmbH, Georg-Westermann-Allee 66, 38104 Braunschweig

ISBN 978-3-14-**121502**-1

Contents

Level of difficulty

●○○ basic | listening comprehension
●●○ intermediate | viewing comprehension
●●● advanced | mediation

PREP & PRACTICE WRITING

PREP & PRACTICE MEDIATION

PREP & PRACTICE EXAMINATION

WES-121502-001 All audio and audio-visual material as well as suggestions for solutions are provided on webcodes. In order to use the webcodes, access the website www.westermann.de/webcode and enter the respective code or scan the QR codes on page 100.

How to work with the Prep & Practice Book

prepare pages give step-by-step information and support on how to work with the material and how to handle the **particular skill**

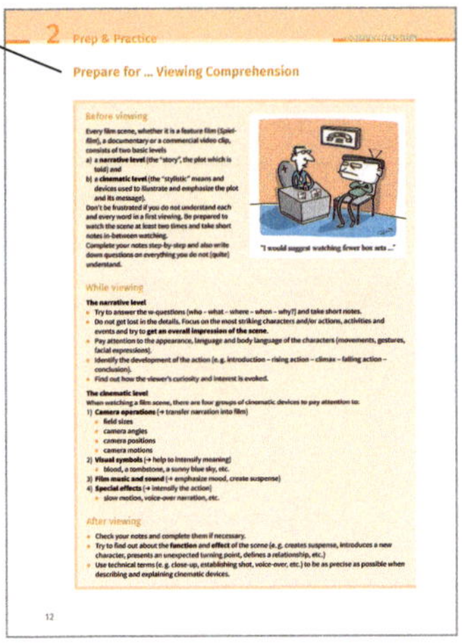

webcodes provide further background information, audio/visual material, and model solutions when you need support or input

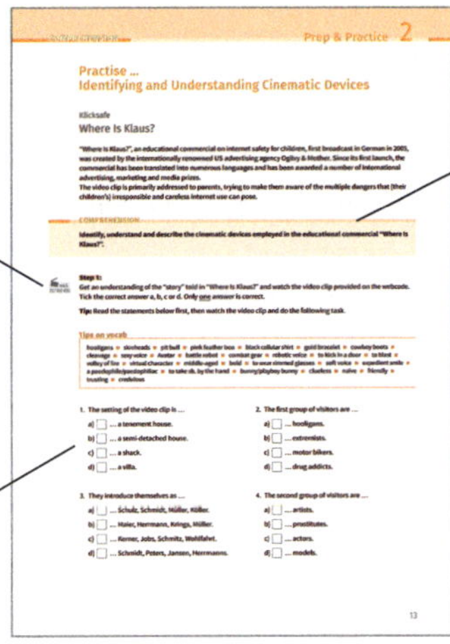

a colour bar indicates that the main **emphasis is on this particular task and skill**; these bars follow the structure of the Students' Book (**comprehension** – **analysis** – **activity**) and point to a detailed step-by-step **guided assignment** on the skill in focus; fully worked-out **solutions** can be found on the **webcode** and accessed via the QR codes on page 100

standardized comprehension formats for reading, listening, or viewing comprehension

additional support in **different colours** on **how to mark** and label relevant keywords/devices/lines in a text

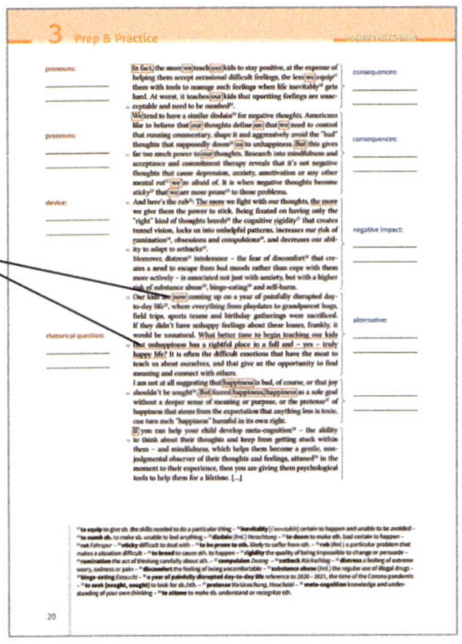

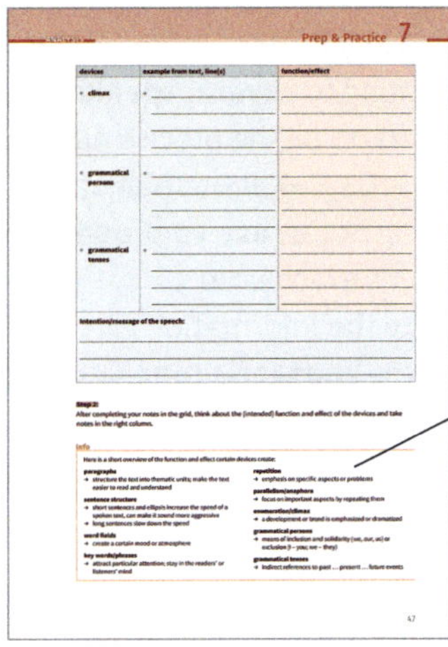

additional background information on the topic or on specific methods help you to complete the tasks independently

notes and further **support** on how to mark a text or material and what to focus on in particular

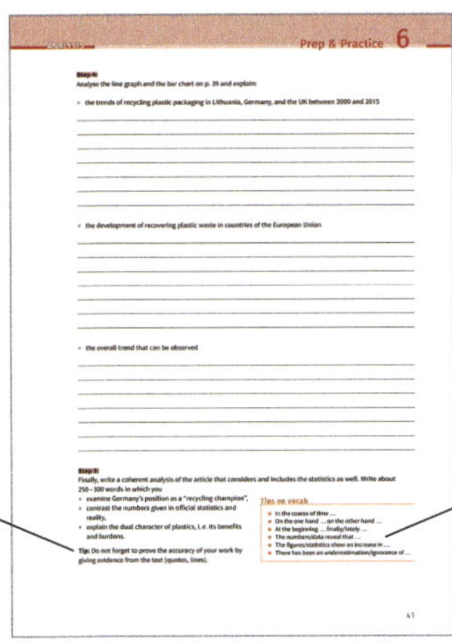

vocab boxes provide language help **for formulations, technical terms,** etc. to do the tasks or to **brush up vocabulary**

annotations and/or **tips on vocab** for each text and the material at hand

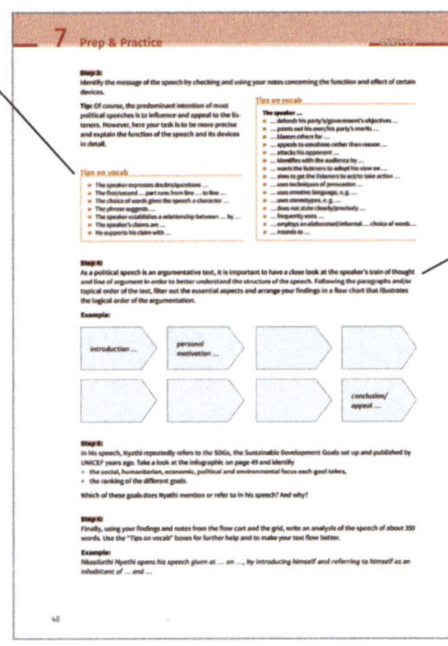

step-by-step tasks provide additional support

Colours used for markings and labellings in the texts:

- content → blue
- stylistic devices → red
- narrative/structural devices → orange
- allusions/symbols/references → green

Prepare for ... Listening Comprehension

Before listening

"You've always been a poor listener Harold."

- Try to **predict** what the text will be about by judging from the title and try to **anticipate** what will be said.
- **Read your listening task** precisely and make sure you understood what you are asked to listen for and pay attention to.

While listening

- Focus on the information in the text that is **relevant to your task** and **leave out irrelevant information**.
- Listen for **keywords** and the **main idea** (the gist) and **do not get distracted in details**.
- Take notes on the **w-questions** (**who** is speaking about **what**, **when**, **where**, and **why**.)
- Note down **key nouns**, names, dates, numbers, times, and places.
- When listening to **several speakers**, try to find out **who they are** and who says what.
- Do not focus on all the precise numbers/data that might be given in a text – **a rough estimate will usually do**, e. g. 53 % → about half of ...
- When taking notes, **use your own words** and **paraphrase** instead of trying to remember and repeat the speaker's exact words.
- **Summarize** the information given using your own words and focusing on the **essentials**.
- Listen for the **speaker's tone and emphasis** of certain words. This can indicate an additional aspect and reveal the **speaker's intention**, e. g. being critical, joking, ironic, appealing, etc.

Using the break

- Use the break before a second listening to **check your notes** and make further additions.
- Check **whether your notes match the given task**.
- Focus on **details in the second listening**.

After listening

- Check if your notes are **logical**.

Try to recapitulate the **context of the text** you listened to and make further additions to your notes.

Practise ... Listening for the Gist and for Details

Emma Watson

HeForShe Campaign Speech at the United Nations

Emma Watson (*1990) is an English actress and activist who has gained international recognition because of her acting role "Hermione Granger" in the *Harry Potter* series. Being an outspoken feminist, Watson was appointed a UN Women Goodwill Ambassador in 2014.
In the course of advocating gender equality, Watson launched the UN women campaign *HeForShe*, which she introduces in the speech at hand.
In 2015, Watson was included in the *TIME 100* list of the world's most influential people. In addition to her feminist activities, Watson has supported the *Black Lives Matter* movement in 2020 and the 2021 UN Climate Change Conference in Glasgow.

COMPREHENSION

Listen to/watch Emma Watson's speech on behalf of the *HeForShe* campaign and outline her remarks on feminism and gender equality.

Tip: The speech can be divided into four thematic units which focus on (slightly) different aspects. Listen to the different parts of the speech one after the other, following the instructions and steps below.

- Part 1: 00:00 – 03:35
- Part 2: 04:03 – 06:40
- Part 3: 06:50 – 08:42
- Part 4: 08:47 – 12:03

Step 1:
Before listening to the speech, do research and collect information about Emma Watson's work as an activist and the various projects she is involved in.

Step 2:
On the basis of your previous research results, try to anticipate what Emma Watson might say about

- her motivation to give the speech

____

____

- her view of how women are treated in society

____

____

- her understanding of gender equality

____

____

WES-121502-001

Step 3:
Now **listen to** Emma Watson's speech, which is provided on the webcode, one part after the other, and try to understand the **gist** (= general meaning) of what is said.
Use your ideas from step 1 and take short notes on what Emma Watson says about these aspects.

Tips on vocab

to launch to start ■ **to galvanize** to cause sb. to suddenly take action, esp. by shocking or exciting them ■ **tangible** real and not imaginary ■ **assumption** *Annahme* ■ **to sexualize** to see sb./sth. in sexual terms ■ **expression** the act of saying what you think ■ **to afford** (*fml.*) to allow sb. to have sth. ■ **inadvertent** not the result of detailed planning ■ **Hillary Clinton** (*1947) American politician, lawyer, and writer who served as United States Secretary of State (2009–2013); she ran for the US presidency in 2016; she is married to Bill Clinton (US President 1993–2001) ■ **to extend** to add to sth. in order to make it bigger or longer ■ **to eclipse sb.** to make another person seem much less important, good, or famous ■ **coronary heart disease** *koronare Herzkrankheit* ■ **distorted** *verzerrt* ■ **to constitute** to be considered as sth. ■ **compelled** *genötigt* ■ **submissive** *unterwürfig* ■ **mantle** the responsibilities of a job ■ **vulnerable** able to be easily hurt ■ **abandoned** left alone and neglected, usually forever ■ **Edmund Burke** (1729–1797) Irish statesman, philosopher and economist

Part 1: 00:00 – 03:35

- the goals of the *HeForShe* campaign

___

___

___

___

- feminism

___

___

___

___

- Emma Watson's personal experiences

___

___

___

___

Part 2: 04:03 – 06:40

- gender equality

___

___

___

___

- Emma Watson's privileged life

- men as feminists

Part 3: 06:50 – 08:42

- men suffering from gender inequality

- gender stereotypes

Part 4: 08:47 – 12:03

- freedom from prejudice

- lack of opportunities for girls and women

Tip: Do not focus on details first; listen for the main idea (e. g. key nouns, names, etc.). Jot down words that you understand and do not bother about words, names, or phrases you do not know.

Step 4:

Listen to the speech **a second time** and try to understand details and more information. **Read the statements below** and decide whether they are true or false. Make corrections to the false statements.

Part 1:

	True	False
1. Watson wants men and boys to be feminists. ___	☐	☐
2. Watson has realized that often feminism goes along with manhating. ___	☐	☐
3. The definition of feminism is that men and women are alike. ___	☐	☐
4. Watson's girlfriends stopped doing sports because they didn't want to get muscular. ___	☐	☐
5. Feminists are often considered to be too strong, too aggressive, isolating and anti-men. ___	☐	☐

Part 2:

	True	False
6. In many countries in the world women receive the same rights as men. ___	☐	☐
7. Watson considers gender equality to be civil rights. ___	☐	☐
8. Many men are reluctant feminists. ___	☐	☐
9. Less than 30 % of the audience listening to Hillary Clinton's famous speech on women's rights were male. ___	☐	☐

Part 3:

	True	False
10. Men are not affected by mental illness or suicide. ___	☐	☐
11. Men have more benefits of equality. ___	☐	☐
12. Many men are aggressive because they want to be accepted. ___	☐	☐
13. Men and women should be able to be strong and sensitive. ___	☐	☐

Part 4:

	True	False
14. *HeForShe* is about freedom from control.	☐	☐
15. Men have the option to make their sons and daughters free from prejudice.	☐	☐
16. Watson appeals to all inadvertent feminists to step forward and become active.	☐	☐

Tip: If necessary, listen to the speech a third time and complete your notes.

Step 5:
Now write an outline of Emma Watson's speech, using your previous notes. Try to use your own words and follow **the introduction – main part – conclusion** pattern.

Write an introductory sentence that answers the w-questions (who – what – where – when – why?). Be careful to use the simple present and indirect speech.

Tip: Have in mind that the comprehension task requires you to focus on Watson's "understanding of feminism and gender equality" and leave out irrelevant details.

Tip: Additionally, remember that the standardized term "outline" requires you to
- work out the main features,
- structure the general principle of a topic,
- omit minor details.

Begin like this: *In a speech, delivered at the United Nations in 2014, the English actress, activist, and UN Women Global Goodwill Ambassador Emma Watson launched the HeForShe campaign and appealed to …*

Tips on vocab

to deliver/give a speech ■ to launch a campaign ■ to ask/call for help/support ■ to include both sides ■ to talk about personal experiences ■ to express/reveal personal feelings/emotions ■ to identify gender stereotypes ■ to fight stereotypes ■ to demand equal rights/treatment ■ to stigmatize sb./sth. ■ to demand respect ■ to enjoy the benefits of sth. ■ to experience a vicious circle of … ■ to take an opportunity ■ to take immediate action ■ to become active

Prepare for ... Viewing Comprehension

Before viewing

Every film scene, whether it is a feature film (*Spielfilm*), a documentary or a commercial video clip, consists of two basic levels

a) a **narrative level** (the "story", the plot which is told) and

b) a **cinematic level** (the "stylistic" means and devices used to illustrate and emphasize the plot and its message).

Don't be frustrated if you do not understand each and every word in a first viewing. Be prepared to watch the scene at least two times and take short notes in-between watching.

Complete your notes step-by-step and also write down questions on everything you do not (quite) understand.

"I would suggest watching fewer box sets ..."

While viewing

The narrative level

- Try to answer the w-questions (who – what – where – when – why?) and take short notes.
- Do not get lost in the details. Focus on the most striking characters and/or actions, activities and events and try to **get an overall impression of the scene**.
- Pay attention to the appearance, language and body language of the characters (movements, gestures, facial expressions).
- Identify the development of the action (e. g. introduction – rising action – climax – falling action – conclusion).
- Find out how the viewer's curiosity and interest is evoked.

The cinematic level

When watching a film scene, there are four groups of cinematic devices to pay attention to:

1) **Camera operations** (→ transfer narration into film)
   - field sizes
   - camera angles
   - camera positions
   - camera motions
2) **Visual symbols** (→ help to intensify meaning)
   - blood, a tombstone, a sunny blue sky, etc.
3) **Film music and sound** (→ emphasize mood, create suspense)
4) **Special effects** (→ intensify the action)
   - slow motion, voice-over narration, etc.

After viewing

- Check your notes and complete them if necessary.
- Try to find out about the **function** and **effect** of the scene (e. g. creates suspense, introduces a new character, presents an unexpected turning point, defines a relationship, etc.)
- Use technical terms (e. g. close-up, establishing shot, voice-over, etc.) to be as precise as possible when describing and explaining cinematic devices.

Practise …
Identifying and Understanding Cinematic Devices

Klicksafe

Where Is Klaus?

"Where Is Klaus?", an educational commercial on internet safety for children, first broadcast in German in 2005, was created by the internationally renowned US advertising agency Ogilvy & Mother. Since its first launch, the commercial has been translated into numerous languages and has been awarded a number of international advertising, marketing and media prizes.
The video clip is primarily addressed to parents, trying to make them aware of the multiple dangers that (their children's) irresponsible and careless internet use can pose.

COMPREHENSION

Identify, understand and describe the cinematic devices employed in the educational commercial "Where Is Klaus?".

WES-121502-002

Step 1:
Get an understanding of the "story" told in "Where Is Klaus?" and watch the video clip provided on the webcode. Tick the correct answer a, b, c or d. Only <u>one</u> answer is correct.

Tip: Read the statements below first, then watch the video clip and do the following task.

Tips on vocab

hooligans ■ skinheads ■ pit bull ■ pink feather boa ■ black cellular shirt ■ gold bracelet ■ cowboy boots ■ cleavage ■ sexy voice ■ Avatar ■ battle robot ■ combat gear ■ robotic voice ■ to kick in a door ■ to blast ■ volley of fire ■ virtual character ■ middle-aged ■ bold ■ to wear rimmed glasses ■ soft voice ■ expedient smile ■ a paedophile/paedophiliac ■ to take sb. by the hand ■ bunny/playboy bunny ■ clueless ■ naive ■ friendly ■ trusting ■ credulous

1. The setting of the video clip is …
   a) ☐ … a tenement house.
   b) ☐ … a semi-detached house.
   c) ☐ … a shack.
   d) ☐ … a villa.

2. The first group of visitors are …
   a) ☐ … hooligans.
   b) ☐ … extremists.
   c) ☐ … motor bikers.
   d) ☐ … drug addicts.

3. They introduce themselves as …
   a) ☐ … Schulz, Schmidt, Müller, Köller.
   b) ☐ … Maier, Herrmann, Krings, Müller.
   c) ☐ … Kerner, Jobs, Schmitz, Wohlfahrt.
   d) ☐ … Schmidt, Peters, Jansen, Herrmanns.

4. The second group of visitors are …
   a) ☐ … artists.
   b) ☐ … prostitutes.
   c) ☐ … actors.
   d) ☐ … models.

5. They want to meet "Klausi" to …
   a) ☐ … have fun with him.
   b) ☐ … seduce him.
   c) ☐ … play games.
   d) ☐ … perform an erotic show.

6. The third visitor is …
   a) ☐ … a toy.
   b) ☐ … an Avatar.
   c) ☐ … a Lego toy.
   d) ☐ … a soldier.

7. He alludes to …
   a) ☐ … Artificial Intelligence.
   b) ☐ … robot toys.
   c) ☐ … violent video/war games.
   d) ☐ … Legoland.

8. The fourth visitor is …
   a) ☐ … a nice neighbour.
   b) ☐ … a friendly uncle.
   c) ☐ … Mom's divorced husband.
   d) ☐ … a paedophile.

9. Mom is …
   a) ☐ … shocked and scared.
   b) ☐ … clueless and trusting.
   c) ☐ … surprised and curious.
   d) ☐ … nervous and excited.

Step 2:
Watch the videoclip a second time and complete your notes.

Step 3:
In order to get a better overview of the plot, watch the video again and find a suitable headline for the various sections.

1. Introduction: ____________________
2. Mom: ____________________
3. ____________________
4. ____________________
5. The front door bursting: ____________________
6. Inside the house: ____________________
7. ____________________
8. Conclusion and message: ____________________

Step 4:
Now, focus on the **cinematic level** and relate the "story" told in the video clip to the images, camera positions, visual symbols, sound effects and special effects used to emphasize its ironic and dramatic effect on the viewer.

Tip: The overall structure of the video clip is very clear and certain images are repeated several times, e. g.
- the front view of the house and approaching car,
- the repeated sequence of Mom opening the front door and different visitors arriving,
- the repeated change between "exterior" (in front of the house) and "interior" (inside the house),
- the focus on four different (groups of) visitors who represent four different potential dangers.

Watch the video clip again and complete the grid.

Tip: There are about 21 parts to the "story".

image	camera position	visual symbol	sound/special effects	potential danger/ message
	*establishing shot*			
	*close-up*			

image	camera position	visual symbol	sound/special effects	potential danger/ message

image	camera position	visual symbol	sound/special effects	potential danger/ message

Step 5:
Finally, using your notes from the previous steps, write a coherent text of about 300 words in which you describe how the combination of narrative and cinematic devices creates the satirical/humourous/surprising/shocking effect on the viewer.

Tip: Do not forget to write an introductory sentence that contains
- the title, type of text, running time of the video clip,
- the author's/director's name,
- the year of release,
- the problem/topic the video clip deals with,
- important characters and features.

Example: *The ironic educational commercial "Where Is Klaus?" released in ... by ... deals with ...*

Your text:

Prepare for ... Reading Comprehension

Before reading

- Be prepared to **read the text at least twice**.
- Depending on the assignment you are given, these two methods help you to get **a quick first overview and understanding**:
  - You can **skim** (= read quickly) the text and try to find main ideas and **most relevant information**.
  - You can **scan** the text and look for a **particular detail** or aspect (key words).
- Reflect on the **headline or title of the text** and try to anticipate what it might be about.

"My reading comprehension is so-so, but I make up for it with my highlighting skills."

While reading

- **Annotate** (= take notes in the margin) the text and **use different colours** for different aspects (see box below).
- **Highlight or underline** relevant or striking key words, names, data, etc.
- **Divide** the text into **paragraphs or thematic units**.
- Give each paragraph or thematic unit **a succinct** (*kurz, bündig*) **and concise** (*prägnant*) **headline**.
- Identify and look up **new vocabulary**.
- **Distinguish facts from opinion** or personal views and comments. Draw a grid in which you list and juxtapose (*gegenüberstellen*) facts and opinions expressed in the text.
- Try to determine the **author's intention** for writing the text.
  - Does he/she want to inform, entertain or appeal to the reader or reflect on an idea?
  - Is he/she objective and balanced (facts, data, expert views) or emotional (emotive language, adjectives) and biased (only one view is presented)?

After reading

- Write down **questions** about words/phrases/aspects you do not understand or are critical about.
- **Cross-check your notes** and focus on the aspects you are required to examine in the assignment. Pay attention to the **Standardized Terminology for Tasks** (*Operatoren*).

Colours used for markings and labellings in the texts:

- content → blue
- stylistic devices → red
- narrative/structural devices → orange
- allusions/symbols/references → green

Practise ... Understanding, Structuring and Summarizing a Non-Fictional Text

Andrea Bonoir

Our Obsession with Happiness Is Making our Kids Miserable

Well-being and wellness have become important factors of how people live and work today. Particularly for Americans, "happiness" has been a key determining factor for the so-called American Way of Life: making the best of everything, looking at life in a positive and optimistic way and strongly believing in anticipated success. The phrase "pursuit of happiness", coined in the Declaration of Independence in 1776, guarantees that Americans can pursue (*verfolgen*) opportunities and have a successful life in their own individual way. However promising this ideal of life may be, the author of the article takes a more critical view, calling it an "obsession", which means that people feel they "have to be" happy even though they don't feel like it.

introduction: ____________ ____________

house rules: ____________ ____________

It was front and center[1] in a slide show of other people's beautiful kitchen renovations: one of those artsy[2] wooden "House Rules" signs. Rule Number 7, showcased[3] in the biggest script of all and sandwiched between "Show compassion" and "Love each other" was this: "BE HAPPY."

reaction: ____________ ____________

Admittedly, seeing that made me anything but[4]. As a psychologist, I can't help but wonder: Who in this world has ever gotten happy because someone else told them they have to be?
And worse, what if our culture's incessant[5] demands to be happy are actually making our kids miserable?
It seems counterintuitive[6], of course, but to be happy in the long run, we should more fully embrace the times when we're not.

US culture: ____________ ____________

In a culture bent on[7] being positive, teaching this mind-set is like swimming upstream. Our kids absorb the "Happy feelings are the most acceptable feelings" message very early on. The smiley-face sticker is the ultimate praise, thinking happy thoughts and turning frowns[8] upside-down[9] make up too many children's songs to count, and the admonition[10] "don't cry" (despite containing no instructions for how to pull this off) has become ubiquitous[11], whether in our attempts to comfort, or our sharp rebukes[12] when our kids' emotional displays[13] frustrate us.

reference: ____________ ____________

____________ ____________ ____________

But this approach to emotional development neglects the full, complicated range of unhappy feelings that are just as valid a part of human life as happiness is – from sadness to frustration, from anger to fear, from guilt to disappointment, boredom or disgust.
Much research on well-being makes clear that Americans' typical approaches to the pursuit of happiness[14] is far from helpful to our kids. Anxiety[15] and mental health problems in children and teens have been steadily increasing, even before the massive disruptions[16] of a year that has been the most difficult of many young lives.

[1] **front and center** very easy to see or notice – [2] **artsy** (*infml., US*) *pseudokünstlerisch* – [3] **to showcase** to show sth. in an attractive way – [4] **anything but** *alles andere als* – [5] **incessant** never stopping, esp. in an unpleasant way – [6] **counterintuitive** *nicht eingängig* – [7] **bent on** *ausgerichtet auf* – [8] **frown** *Stirnrunzeln* – [9] **to turn sth. upside-down** *etw. umkehren, auf den Kopf stellen* – [10] **admonition** warning – [11] **ubiquitous** [juːˈbɪkwɪtəs] (*fml.*) seeming to be everywhere – [12] **rebuke** (*fml.*) *Rüge* – [13] **emotional display** negative outburst of stubbornness – [14] **pursuit of happiness** the act of achieving a plan or fulfilling a dream – [15] **anxiety** [æŋˈzaɪəti] a feeling of nervousness or worry – [16] **disruption** an interruption in the usual way that sth. works

pronouns: ____________

consequences: ____________

In fact, the more we teach our kids to stay positive, at the expense of helping them accept occasional difficult feelings, the less we equip[17] them with tools to manage such feelings when life inevitably[18] gets hard. At worst, it teaches our kids that upsetting feelings are unacceptable and need to be numbed[19].

pronouns: ____________

consequences: ____________

We tend to have a similar disdain[20] for negative *thoughts*. Americans like to believe that our thoughts define us: that we need to control that running commentary, shape it and aggressively avoid the "bad" thoughts that supposedly doom[21] us to unhappiness. But this gives far too much power to our thoughts. Research into mindfulness and acceptance and commitment therapy reveals that it's not negative thoughts that cause depression, anxiety, amotivation or any other mental rut[22] we're afraid of. It is when negative thoughts become *sticky*[23] that we are more prone[24] to those problems.

device: ____________

negative impact: ____________

And here's the rub[25]: The more we fight with our thoughts, the more we give them the power to stick. Being fixated on having only the "right" kind of thoughts breeds[26] the cognitive rigidity[27] that creates tunnel vision, locks us into unhelpful patterns, increases our risk of rumination[28], obsessions and compulsions[29], and decreases our ability to adapt to setbacks[30].

Moreover, distress[31] intolerance – the fear of discomfort[32] that creates a need to escape from bad moods rather than cope with them more actively – is associated not just with anxiety, but with a higher risk of substance abuse[33], binge-eating[34] and self-harm.

rhetorical question: ____________

alternative: ____________

Our kids are now coming up on a year of painfully disrupted day-to-day life[35], where everything from playdates to grandparent hugs, field trips, sports teams and birthday gatherings were sacrificed. If they didn't have unhappy feelings about these losses, frankly, it would be unnatural. What better time to begin teaching our kids that unhappiness has a rightful place in a full and – yes – truly happy life? It is often the difficult emotions that have the most to teach us about ourselves, and that give us the opportunity to find meaning and connect with others.

____

I am not at all suggesting that happiness is bad, of course, or that joy shouldn't be sought[36]. But forced happiness, happiness as a sole goal without a deeper sense of meaning or purpose, or the pretense[37] of happiness that stems from the expectation that anything less is toxic, can turn such "happiness" harmful in its own right.

If you can help your child develop meta-cognition[38] – the ability to think about their thoughts and keep from getting stuck within them – and mindfulness, which helps them become a gentle, nonjudgmental observer of their thoughts and feelings, attuned[39] in the moment to their experience, then you are giving them psychological tools to help them for a lifetime. [...]

[17] **to equip** to give sb. the skills needed to do a particular thing – [18] **inevitably** [ɪˈnevɪtəblɪ] certain to happen and unable to be avoided – [19] **to numb sb.** to make sb. unable to feel anything – [20] **disdain** (*fml.*) *Verachtung* – [21] **to doom** to make sth. bad certain to happen – [22] **rut** *Fahrspur* – [23] **sticky** difficult to deal with – [24] **to be prone to sth.** likely to suffer from sth. – [25] **rub** (*fml.*) a particular problem that makes a situation difficult – [26] **to breed** to cause sth. to happen – [27] **rigidity** the quality of being impossible to change or persuade – [28] **rumination** the act of thinking carefully about sth. – [29] **compulsion** *Zwang* – [30] **setback** *Rückschlag* – [31] **distress** a feeling of extreme worry, sadness or pain – [32] **discomfort** the feeling of being uncomfortable – [33] **substance abuse** (*fml.*) the regular use of illegal drugs – [34] **binge-eating** *Esssucht* – [35] **a year of painfully disrupted day-to-day life** reference to 2020–2021, the time of the Corona pandemic – [36] **to seek (sought, sought)** to look for sb./sth. – [37] **pretense** *Vortäuschung, Heuchelei* – [38] **meta-cognition** knowledge and understanding of your own thinking – [39] **to attune** to make sb. understand or recognize sth.

Talk about true happiness as more than just pleasure or ease[40]. We all want our kids to be happy. But what they absorb about what that means is crucial. By opening them up to the idea of a sense of purpose, finding meaning in their life, or defining the values important to them, they will have a better understanding of how even challenging, difficult times can cultivate happiness. Be aware of the ways that you put external, superficial definitions of happiness – like acing a test or winning a championship – above the internal sense of pride that comes from working hard on something that matters to your child.

true happiness:

____

____

conclusion:

____

____

Soon, they (and you) will be more open to the true experience of happiness – and whatever else life brings.

consequences:

____

____

https://www.washingtonpost.com/lifestyle/2021/02/23/kids-happiness-emotions, 23 February 2021 [02.04.2021]

COMPREHENSION

Summarize the newspaper article about "obsessive happiness" and point out the consequences this can have for children and teenagers.

Step 1:
In a **first reading**, clarify unknown words and phrases and try to get a **general understanding** of what the author criticizes.

Step 2:
Read the article **a second time** and subdivide it into paragraphs following the thematic units. Mark the paragraphs in the margin of the page and jot down some key words.

Tip: Do not only follow the print pattern! If you have difficulties in paragraphing, pay attention to changes and breaks as described in the box below.

Info

Paragraphs subdivide a text into manageable portions and help organize meaning. Often, each paragraph is organized around a central idea or key word which is usually made clear in the first sentence or phrase. Paragraphs follow each other in a successive order and take the reader from a to b to c, usually linked by connectives or phrases. In a **non-fictional text**, a new paragraph can indicate:
- a change in the line of argument,
- the introduction of an additional aspect or topic,
- a counter-argument or another supportive argument,
- the presentation of an example.

Step 3:
Find a suitable headline for each paragraph using your previous notes and your own words.

line(s)	headline
1 – 5	*The Home Rule: Be Happy*
	What if …?

[40] **ease** *Leichtigkeit*

	Being open to …

Step 4:
Before writing a summary, make sure that you have understood everything correctly. Do the reading comprehension task and take short notes on the questions below.

- What makes the author critical about "being happy all the time"?

____

____

____

____

- What, according to the author, is most important in American culture?

____

____

____

____

- What are the assumed or alleged negative consequences?

____

____

____

____

- What would be a better alternative?

____

____

____

____

Step 5:
Finally, write a summary of the article in about 250 words, using your previous notes.

Tip:
- Do not forget to use the simple present as your basic time.
- Write an introductory sentence that answers the w-questions (who – what – where – when – why?).
- Use your own words and employ introductory formulations to make your text more fluent and vary the beginnings of your sentences.

Tips on vocab

The author criticizes that … ■ In addition, the author expresses doubts/questions … ■ Further on, the author states that … ■ The author has personally experienced how … ■ She continues arguing that …

Example: *In her article "Our Obsession with Happiness Is Making our Kids Miserable", the author Andrea Bonoir reflects on and criticizes the American habit of …*

Your summary:

Prepare for ... Reading Comprehension

A **narrative text**, like a novel or short story, belongs to the category of **fiction**, i. e. literature written by an author that describes imaginary events and people. Fiction is commonly **written in prose**, which is written or spoken language in its ordinary form that flows in natural patterns of everyday speech.
Major elements which are employed in fiction can be details such as character(s), plot, point of view, setting, style, theme and conflict. Most authors also employ elements of imagery (*Bildsprache*) such as leitmotifs and metaphors in their works.

Before reading

- On the basis of the cover, blurb (*Klappentext*) or title of the novel or story, imagine or anticipate what the topic(s) might be.
- If possible, do research on the novel or story and try to form a synopsis of the plot to get a first overview.

While reading

- **Annotate** (= make notes in the margin) the text and use different colours for different aspects (see box below).
- After reading the introductory part (= exposition) **take notes on the w-questions**:
  - who: characters, protagonist
  - where/when: setting (= time + place)
  - what: topic, events or problem(s) to be expected
  - why: assumed intention or message
- Try to **identify the point-of-view** (narrative perspective), e. g. first-person narrator, third-person narrator, omniscient narrator, etc.
- Take **notes on (relevant) thoughts or ideas** the (main) character(s) express(es).
  - What is their point of view?
  - Which problems do they have to face or deal with?
- Do not forget to note the page(s) or line(s) where you found the information.
- Find out about **hints given about past** (flashback) or **future** (foreshadowing) events that might be important.

After reading

- Sort and structure your notes as you might need them for your analysis later on.

Colours used for markings and labellings in the texts:

- content → blue
- stylistic devices → red
- narrative/structural devices → orange
- allusions/symbols/references → green

Practise ... Reading and Understanding a Narrative Text

John Corey Whaley

Where Things Come Back

The 17-year-old first-person narrator and protagonist of John Corey Whaley's 2011 coming-of-age novel, Cullen Winter, is a high school senior in Lily, a small town in Arkansas. Cullen sees his hometown as a place where "dreams go to die" and nothing ever happens – which is why he longs to get away to somewhere more exciting and less lonely and isolated.
Ada Taylor, the girl he is attracted to, is one grade above Cullen and the most beautiful girl in school. However, there seems to a bad spell around her: all her boyfriends die (in tragic accidents) after some time ... Cullen feels being left out and alone which is supported by the situation of being bullied by a boy called Russell Quitman and his friends.

narrator: ______

stream of consciousness: ______ ______

language: ______ ______

life: ______ ______

Cullen Winter: ______ ______

Ada: ______ ______

Being seventeen and bored in a small town, I like to pretend sometimes that I'm a pessimist. *This is the way it is and nothing can sway*[1] *me from that. Life sucks most of the time. Everything is bullshit. High school sucks*[2]*. You go to school, work for fifty years, then you die.* Only I can't seem to keep that up for too long before my natural urge[3] to idealize goes into effect. I can't seem to be a pessimist long enough to overlook the possibility of things being overwhelmingly good. [...] Like most teenage boys, I, Cullen Winter, was in love with a beautiful girl who had a big, burly[4] boyfriend who would just as soon kick my ass[5] as look at me. His name was Russell Quitman, and I didn't care too much for his brother or parents, either. But I sometimes dislike people by association[6]. The girl's name was Ada Taylor, and she could have probably kicked my ass too. (If you haven't figured it out yet, just about everyone you know could probably kick my ass.) If you lived in Lily, Arkansas, which we all did, then you knew Ada, or at least knew about her. I'm pretty sure even some of the kids in Little Rock[7] and Memphis[8] heard stories about Lily's own black widow[9].
You see, Ada Taylor had a grim history. As a sophomore[10] in high school, when I was just a freshman, Ada was dating a senior and made it his personal mission to make every freshman in the school terrified to be caught walking alone or near the bathrooms, lockers, or trash cans. But alas, he died before Christmas break in a car accident. Ada was the only other passenger. She walked away without a scratch. Then, the next year, Ada was dating this okay guy who I used to play G.I. Joes with on the floor of my mom's hair salon. His name was Aaron Lancaster. He didn't even make it to Thanksgiving before he up and drowned[11] in the White River during a thunderstorm. His dad found his empty fishing boat. A search party found his body four days later. I heard it looked like he had been microwaved.
After that, it almost seemed like a ridiculous thing to date Ada Taylor, or even go near her. But that didn't matter much to the young men of Lily, even me. The unspoken philosophy of all those in love with Ada was something like this: If I have to die to get that, then death it is.

[1] **to sway** to cause sth. to change – [2] **to suck** (*offensive, US*) to be bad or unpleasant – [3] **urge** *Drang* – [4] **burly** large and strong – [5] **kick my ass** (*offensive, US*) to punish or defeat sb. with a lot of force – [6] **by association** through a relation to sb./sth. – [7] **Little Rock** a town in the US state of Arkansas – [8] **Memphis** a town in the US state of Tennessee – [9] **black widow** a very poisonous spider that kills the male spider after having sex with it – [10] **sophomore** a student in the second grade of high school (grade 10) – [11] **to up and drown** (*sl., US*) to suddenly die by drowning (*Ertrinken*)

But there we were with one week of school left and Russell Quitman was still breathing up all the air around him and taking up all the extra table space around him in the lunchroom with his monstrous biceps. I had bet Lucas that Russell wouldn't last past Easter. That cost me ten bucks. You might think it sadistic to bet on an eighteen-year-old boy's death or to talk about it like I wanted it to happen or something. This would just further prove that you'd never met Russell Quitman. Certain people are supposed to be the ones who burn up in fiery[12] crashes or drown in the rapids of a river in the middle of the night. These are the Russell Quitmans of the world. [...]

I called Russell the Quit Man for two reasons. The first one was obvious, list last name. That's a no-brainer[13]. But the other reason I called him this was much more related to his character. It was because the most frequent thing heard when near Russell Quitman were the cries of whatever prey[14] he was putting into a headlock[15] or holding upside down or tripping in the hallway. "Quit, man. Quit!" How is it that Russell Quitman, the Quit Man, could be so cruel, such a huge douche bag[16], and still manage to go out with the prettiest girl in town? I call this the Pretty Paradox. Pretty girls always want guys who treat them, and most everyone else, like complete shit. It is perhaps one of the most baffling phenomena in history. Book Title #72: *Good Things Happen to Bad People.*

I'm not sure why anything like the existence of the Quit Man or girls liking him surprised me in a place like Lily. Living in Lily, Arkansas, is sometimes like living in the land that time forgot. We do have things like Burger King and McDonald's, and we even have a Walmart, but if you are looking for much more than this, you'll must have to keep on driving through. Like most Arkansas towns, Lily does have an abundance of one thing: trees. Lily is all trees and dirt sliced into circles by curved roads. Lily is also water, though. The White River runs right along the edge of town and all the way across the state and over to the Mississippi.

If you've ever been to Lily, and I bet you haven't, then you need to know that it is located almost exactly halfway between Little Rock and Memphis. There are 3,947 people, according to the faded green sign on the side of the road as you drive into town, and most of those people are complete ass-hats[17] who tried and subsequently failed to leave this place behind. One unique thing about Lily is that, for a small town in the middle of nowhere, it seems to be very clean, well-kept sort of place. Lily is the kind of place you'd like to move to some short time before you die. If at any other time in your life you think you need the peace and quiet of Lily, Arkansas, then you should either see a therapist or stay there for a week and try to find anything half-entertaining to do.

from *Where Things Come Back* by John Corey Whaley. Atheneum, New York 2011, pp. 5 ff.

reference: ______

pun: ______

Russell Quitman: ______

Lily: ______

[12] **fiery** ['faɪəri] full of extremely bright flames – [13] **no-brainer** (*infml.*) sth. that is very easy or obvious – [14] **prey** *Beute* – [15] **headlock** *Schwitzkasten* – [16] **douche bag** (*offensive, US*) an unpleasant person – [17] **ass-hat** (*offensive, US*) *Arschloch*

COMPREHENSION

Describe Cullen Winter's situation, his view of life and the various problems he has to deal with.

Step 1:
Read the first two paragraphs of the excerpt and highlight the key words and dominant phrases.
What information is given about:
- the narrator or the point of view,
- the setting (time + place),
- the topic of the novel,
- the situation Cullen is (caught) in?

Step 2:
Against the background of your previous findings and clues given in these first paragraphs, speculate on
- how the action might develop and
- which (further) complications might occur.

____

____

____

____

____

Step 3:
Read the **third and fourth paragraph** (l. 18 – l. 33) and take notes on what the narrator tells about:

- Ada Taylor:

____

____

____

____

- Ada's boyfriends:

____

____

____

____

- loving Ada:

____

____

____

____

Step 4:
After reading the next paragraphs (l. 34 – l. 54), take notes on Russell Quitman:

- Russel, the bully:

____
____
____
____

- Russell and Ada:

____
____
____
____

- the Pretty Paradox:

____
____
____
____

Step 5:
In the following paragraphs (l. 55 – l. 77), the narrator describes his hometown, Lily. After reading these paragraphs, take notes on these aspects:

- Lily's infrastructure:

____
____
____
____

- Lily's geography:

____
____
____
____

- moving to Lily:

____
____
____
____

Step 6:
Read the excerpt a **second time** and collect the information given about the narrator Cullen Winter's description and view of Ada, Russell Quitman and Lily. Complete the grid below.

Ada Taylor	Russell Quitman	Lily
• *a beautiful girl*	• *big, burly*	• *the land that time forgot*
• *black widow*	•	•
•	•	•
•	•	•
•	•	•
•	•	•
•	•	•
•	•	•
•	•	•

Tip: Use a dictionary to find suitable adjectives and phrases that describe the characters as well as Cullen's emotions.

Example:
Ada: promiscuous, sexy, …
Russell: brutal, ruthless, …
Lily: boring, bourgeois (spießig), …

Step 7:
After having gained an overview of the situation and the relevant characters, write a coherent text of about 300 words in which you give an account of Cullen's situation and the problems he has to deal with.

Tip: Do not forget to begin your description with an introductory sentence which contains
- the name of the author,
- the title of the novel,
- the place and date of publication,
- the character's situation,
- a short (!) presentation of the plot and the central idea of the story.

Example:
The excerpt at hand, taken from the novel … by …, published …, depicts the protagonist's views and reflections on …

Your text:

____

____

____

____

____

____

____

____

Prepare for ... Analysis of a Fictional Text

Before analysing

Whenever you are asked to analyse a fictional text, i. e. an excerpt from a novel or short story, the assignment you are given will focus on a particular part or element that has to be dealt with specifically.
You can be asked to

- **characterize** somebody (e.g. the protagonist) or something (e. g. a situation, problem, an event, an attitude, etc.),
- **identify** and **explain** the **narrative devices** and their function and effect (e. g. inner monologue, stream of consciousness, etc.),
- **examine** the **structural devices** (e. g. breaks, foreshadowing, flashbacks, etc.),
- **analyse** the **style** and/or specific **use of language** (e. g. choice of words, word field, language register, etc.).

Therefore it is important to pay attention to the exact wording of the assignment (*Operatoren*) and what exactly it requires you to focus on.

While analysing

- Identify the **narrator** and specify what **point of view** is being used to tell the story.
- Take notes in the margin of the text using different colours (see box below) and highlight/underline important keywords and phrases in the text.
- Pay attention to the **mode of presentation** (e. g. scenic, panoramic) and how it supports the development of the events/situation described in the text.

After analysing

- Keep in mind that an analysis requires you to examine and explain (devices in) a text. Be careful not to evaluate or comment on your findings.
  In a **written analysis** you are required to write a **coherent text** in which you connect your findings with regard to a certain function and effect that specific devices achieve.
  In order to formulate and work out your results as precisely as possible, use the **3-step** method:
  1) use the **correct technical term** for the device
  2) present a **quote** from the text and give the number of the **lines** where you found it
  3) explain the **function and effect** of the device
- As an analysis requires precision and a matter-of-fact style of writing, use the **simple present** as the predominant tense.

Colours used for markings and labellings in the texts:

- content → blue
- stylistic devices → red
- narrative/structural devices → orange
- allusions/symbols/references → green

Practise ... Analysing an Excerpt from a Novel

Callan Wink

August

The protagonist of the novel, August, lives on his parents' dairy farm in rural Michigan. The novel covers August's adolescence from the age of twelve to nineteen. After his parents' divorce, his mother takes on a job as a librarian in Montana, taking August with her, and August tries to cope with the new situation and environment there.

narrative perspective:

____

____

topic:

____

mother's plans:

____

____

That spring, August took the SAT[1] and did well enough. It wasn't long before the college brochures started flooding the mailbox. He didn't give them much more than a glance, but one morning he came downstairs before school and found his mother flipping through the pile[2], drinking coffee. "Oh, look at this one, St. Lawrence University, in upstate New York; it looks beautiful. Or how about the University of California, in Santa Cruz? Right in the redwoods[3], maybe you could learn how to surf. Oh, hey, here's Dartmouth, that's flattering, I mean, *Ivy League*[4], Augie wouldn't that be something?"

"Just because they sent me a brochure doesn't mean they would actually let me in. Surfing," he shook his head. "I don't see it."

"This summer we need to visit a school or two, at the very least. It's hard to get a feel for these places unless you walk the campus, see the lay of the land, meet some students. I think it will be fun."

August was at the sink pouring cereal into a bowl. "I told Dad I'd come work for him again this summer," he said. He went to the fridge for the milk, not looking at his mother. She was silent, and he didn't have to look at her to know her face: jaw set[5], eyes narrowed. He started to eat, still standing with his back to her, feeling her stare.

____

____

____

"What?" he said. "I told him I'd come back to work, and he's counting on it. I can't change my mind at the last second."

His mother rose and walked over to stand next to him. She put her mug in the sink, and he could smell the coffee on her breath, smoke from her morning cigarillo in her hair. "Your father doesn't need your help in that goddamn barn," she said. "He needs you around so he can feel like his life hasn't been a complete waste. I'm going to work now but we're not done discussing this."

mode of presentation:

____

____

There were many more discussions. Fights. Long spells[6] where he and his mother barely exchanged words. And, in the end, there was one more humid green Michigan summer. A summer tallied[7] in fountain Cokes[8] and the slow accumulation of $7.50 hours. Cicadas[9] droning in the poplars, sticky nights with the windows open, the heat lightning crackling the black eggshell of sky. All the girls in town and none of them his. The stink of manure[10], hay itch[11], the sharp line of tanned skin right at the point of his short sleeves stopped. Baseball and sun tea. [...] There were no college visits.

[1] **SAT** (*abbr.*) Scholastic Aptitude Test, a standardized test to measure academic success – [2] **pile** *Stapel* – [3] **redwood** *Mammutbaum* – [4] **Ivy League** a group of eight respected colleges and universities in the Northeast of the US, e.g. Harvard, Yale – [5] **to set your jaw** *das Kinn anspannen* – [6] **spell** a period of time – [7] **to tally** to count – [8] **fountain Coke** Coke that is tapped from a soda fountain (machine) and not served in a bottle – [9] **cicadas** *Zikade, Heuschrecke* – [10] **manure** *Dung* – [11] **hay itch** an allergic reaction of the skin to hay and pollen

At the airport, the day of his departure, his father shook his hand and heaved his bag out of the truck. "Thanks for all the help this summer," he said. "Couldn't have done it without you. Senior year," he said, giving it a low whistle. "Hard to imagine. Enjoy it. Next summer we'll talk about bringing you on board on a more permanent basis. No more hourly wage. I was thinking more of a partnership, a profit-sharing kind of deal – what do you think?"

Dad's plans:

____

____

August shouldered is bag, watched a jet taxiing[12] down the runway behind his father's shoulder.

"Sure," he said. "Yeah, maybe. We'll see what happens."

When he returned to Montana he told his mother he'd apply to Montana State in Bozeman for the next year. He'd thought about it over the summer. He knew he could get a good scholarship, and he didn't want to accumulate debt. She told him that she respected his decision. "MSU[13] is not a bad school at all, and you'll be close, so that will be nice. I kind of like having you around." [...]

Whenever his father called, he made sure to let August know that if he didn't go to college he'd need to be finding a job, and that he had plenty of work for him if he decided to come back. He never came right out and said that he was struggling to get everything done around the place, but August could tell that he wanted him to think that was the case. [...]

August was still fighting with her about college. At this point, continuing with school seemed like handing his mother a victory in the ill-defined[14] battle they been engaged [...]. She'd called the Montana State registrar[15] and was furious when they told her no application had been filed under his name. He'd instead decided that he wanted to be a wildlands firefighter or possibly go work in the Wyoming oil fields, like Gaskill's older brother, who'd returned to town with a brand-new truck. Said he was going back and could get August on.

reference:

____

____

This was two years after 9/11 and the military recruiters[16] still came to August's high school at least once a week, smelling blood. As a senior August could sign up for the National Guard and they'd give him four thousand dollars just as soon as he passed the test. *Put your name in, they'd say, just a few years, and then when you get out we'll pay for your school. You want to go to college, son, don't you? Of course you do. But how are you going to pay for that? You're an upstanding[17] young man, I can tell. You expect your parents to foot[18] the bill? Are you going to take out loans[19]?*

military recruiting:

____

____

August saw through the whole game pretty quickly. Probably thanks to his mother, he had to admit. She still spent weekends with Art, but on weeknights she made August watch Bill O'Reilly[20] with her. She'd sit on the couch, smoking, emitting the small noise of disgust with each drag. When she show was over, she'd switch off the TV, mix herself a drink, and tune in the radio to the NPR[21] station out of Billings. They'd sit in silence and listen to the BBC World News. She never said anything, allowing him to formulate his own opinions.

[12] **to taxi** to move slowly on the ground – [13] **MSU** (*abbr.*) Michigan State University – [14] **ill-defined** not clearly described or shown – [15] **registrar** an official whose job is to keep official records, esp. of births, marriages, etc. – [16] **military recruiter** a person who persuades people to enter the military – [17] **upstanding** behaving in a good and moral way – [18] **to foot sth.** (*infml.*) to pay an amount of money – [19] **loan** *Darlehen, Kredit* – [20] **Bill O'Reilly** (*1949) American journalist, TV host and political commentator – [21] **NPR** (*abbr.*) National Public Radio; an American non-profit media organization

August didn't figure that there was much formulating in him at all until Ramsay got blown up. He had four younger brothers. His mother weighed three hundred pounds and hardly ever left the house. His old man drove long-haul[22] trucks, only came home every couple of weeks. Ramsay had been smart enough to go to college anywhere, for free, probably, but he had to do the weekly grocery shopping for his mom, had to clean up after his brothers. In other words, he wasn't listening to BBC World News on NPR. He'd taken the four thousand dollars. He'd come back from that first deployment with burns over 70 percent of his body and died at a military hospital somewhere in Texas. August still couldn't quite figure out what exact part of a National Guardsman's duty involved riding in a Hummer in Afghanistan. The brochures the recruiting officers gave out showed smiling young men and women in fatigues[23] handing one another sandbags while flood-stricken[24] locals stood by, gratitude[25] written all over their faces.

After Ramsay, everything seemed desperate somehow. It was as if August and all the guys he knew had caught something. One of their own would never be coming back, and that first encounter with the enemy, that taste of mortality[26], had left everyone a bit unhinged[27]. [...]

August put down his bag and sat. His boot was tipping on the floor. He'd make it stop and then it would start again without him even realizing it.

"Are you going somewhere?"

He'd planned on telling her that he was just taking some clothes and stuff over to the ranch. But he'd never lied much to his mom. "I guess so," he said.

"Are you going back to be with your dad?"

August could see how much it took for her to ask this question.

"Nah, I think I'm going in the other direction."

"Okay. Because I'd understand if you wanted to do that. I'm not saying you shouldn't."

"It's fine, Mom, I'm not going back there."

"What about school this fall?"

"I don't think it's for me."

"So you've thought about it, really thought about it?"

"I have. Seems like something people do to put off actually doing something."

"And that's your conclusion?"

"For now."

from *August* by Callan Wink. Granta Publications, New York 2020, pp. 89 ff.

sarcasm: __________

mode of presentation: __________

Ramsay's death: __________

brochures: __________

decision: __________

COMPREHENSION

In preparation of the analysis, **read the excerpt** one or two times and pay attention to

- the structure of the text,
- the presentation of the protagonist and the other characters,
- relevant events.

Highlight and/or underline the respective words and phrases in the text and take notes in the margin of the text.

[22] **long-haul** travelling a long distance – [23] **fatigues** [fəˈtiːg] military uniform worn in the field – [24] **flood-stricken** suffering severely from the effects of a flood – [25] **gratitude** thankfulness – [26] **mortality** *Sterblichkeit* – [27] **unhinged** mentally ill

ANALYSIS

Examine the narrative perspective and narrative technique employed in the excerpt and explain how they support the indirect characterization of the protagonist, August.

Tip: Before you underline and/or highlight further parts of the text, make sure that you have understood the complex analysis task. Pay attention to relevant keywords in the assignment which show what exactly to focus on.

Info

Narrative technique/narrative perspective:

- **point of view:** the perspective from which the characters or events are presented
- **unlimited point of view/omniscient narrator:** a narrator who knows everything; presents the action and the characters' thoughts, etc.
- **imited point of view:** e. g. a first-person or third-person narrator who only has limited insight
- **witness/observer narrator:** a narrator who is a character in the story (e. g. protagonist or minor character); usually has a limited perspective
- **subjective/unreliable or objective/reliable narrator:** a narrator whom the reader can(not) trust, e. g. because they are (dis)honest
- **stream of consciousness:** the presentation of experiences and thoughts through the mind (→ thoughts) of one character in a text (→ *erlebte Rede*); a special technique here is the **interior monologue** (= a special kind of **scenic presentation** which is often not ordered or logical)
- **mode of presentation:**
  a) **panoramic** → the author tells the story …
  b) **scenic:** → the author shows an event in detail using dialogue and describing a scene, etc.

Info

Direct characterization:

- the playwright tells the audience what the character's personality is like, e. g. in the stage directions
- one of the other characters refers to/explains/talks about a character's personality

Indirect characterization:

- the playwright shows the character talking and acting which reveals his/her personality
- a character's personality may be revealed through his/her a) speech, b) thoughts, c) effect on others, d) actions, and e) looks/appearance

Step 1:
In a first step, identify and determine the **narrative perspective/point of view** that is used in the excerpt. Here are some questions that help you to identify the point of view:

- Is the narrator part of the events?
- What does the narrator know about the other characters and their thoughts, emotions, etc.?
- How does the narrator present the events?
- Does the narrator interfere or add comments?
- When is the narrative technique of "stream of consciousness" employed in the text?

Step 2:
Collect information given in the excerpt about how August thinks about and reacts to these aspects:

aspect/event	August's thoughts and reaction
college brochures 	______ ______ ______

his mother's plans 	
his father's plans 	
military recruiters 	
Ramsay's death 	

Step 3:
Find examples of the different modes of presentation employed throughout the excerpt.
Is there one predominant mode of presentation – and if so, what is the function and effect?

Step 4:
Specify how August's behaviour, thoughts, and reflections as well as his reactions/replies to his parents indirectly characterize him.
Use the examples given in the grid and complete it.

August's behaviour/thought/reply	indirect characterization
• He didn't give them much more than a glance.	→ *August is not interested in college at all*
• … he shook his head. "I don't see it."	→
• "I told Dad I'd come …"	→
• … he didn't have to look at her to know her face …	→
• All the girls in town and none of them his.	→
• "We'll see what happens."	→
•	→
•	→

Step 5:
Finally, using your previous notes and considerations, explain how August is indirectly characterized by the use of certain narrative techniques.
Write a coherent text of about 300 words and use the **introduction – main part – conclusion** pattern for your text.

Prepare for ... Analysis of a Non-Fictional Text

Before analysing

- Brush up your (background) knowledge of the topic(s) the article deals with.
- If possible, do some research on the respective matter and take notes on aspects, possible problems or recent trends connected with it.

While analysing

- Determine the **type of text**:
  a) Does the author want to **inform** in a balanced and neutral way?
  b) Does the author try to **influence** the reader (directly/indirectly)?
  c) Is the text **argumentative**, **scientific** or **descriptive**?
  d) Is the **source** of the text credible?
- Divide the text into **paragraphs** and relate them to the **heading**.
- Determine the **message** of the text.
- Clarify the **line of argument** (the train of thought in the text).
- Do not forget to include **quotes**.
- Use the **simple present** for your analysis.
- Your task is to analyse in a matter-of-fact way. Therefore, avoid (personal) evaluations and judgements – stay objective. The results of your analysis should be based on the text and not on personal judgement.

Analysing statistical data

- Use the correct technical term for the statistics, e. g.
  - table/grid,
  - line graph,
  - bar chart,
  - pie chart.
- Focus on **striking and/or obvious differences**, **trends** and **developments**.
- **Compare different data** and/or years to each other and show the development or change that has taken place.
- Refer to striking lows or peaks as well as (sudden) rises or drops in a development.
- Consider why a bar chart, graph or table has been chosen as the means of illustration.
- **Relate the data to** the **given context**.

Colours used for markings and labellings in the texts:

- content → blue
- stylistic devices → red
- narrative/structural devices → orange
- allusions/symbols/references → green

Practise ... Examining a Newspaper/Magazine Article and Statistical Data

Katharina Wecker

Plastic Waste and the Recycling Myth

Plastic is considered to be a benefit and a burden at the same time. It has many advantages and has made our modern way of life possible over the last decades. But, unfortunately, plastic poses a great danger to our environment and health. It literally never disappears and the world seems to be suffocating from plastic trash and unable to handle the problem.

Germany is hailed[1] worldwide as a recycling champion. But like many European countries, it actually recycles a lot less plastic packaging waste than commonly understood – with dire[2] consequences for the environment.

Recycling is nearly a national pastime[3] in Germany. There's a blue bin for paper, a brown or green bin for biodegradables, a yellow one for plastic and a black one for the rest.

Additionally, Germans return their deposit bottles to the supermarket, and drop glass bottles at public collecting points.

Germans are proud of their recycling system. Even children's books spin the tale[4] of the colored bins.

Indeed, the nation is celebrated as a recycling role model around the world. When Germany introduced its recycling system with the "green dot" as a symbol in 1991, it was unparalleled[5].

Today, 29 European countries along with Israel and Turkey have adopted the green-dot system, where companies pay a fee to finance the collection, sorting and recovery of packaging waste.

And Germany retains[6] its good reputation. In 2017, the World Economic Forum named the country recycling world champion.

The "green dot" has become an international symbol for the collection of packaging waste.

Yet experts argue that Germany doesn't actually recycle as much waste as statistics suggest – especially when it comes to plastic packaging.

Germany: ________________

choice of words: ________________

Collecting is not recycling

Globally, we generate[7] about 1.3 billion tons of trash per year. In Germany alone, this amounts to a whopping[8] 3 million tons of plastic packaging waste annually.

According to official statistics, 48.8 percent of that plastic waste was recycled in Germany.

But that figure is deceptive[9], says Philipp Sommer, a circular economy expert with the German environmental and consumer protection association Deutsche Umwelthilfe (DUH).

"We assume that only 38 percent was actually recycled," he told DW.

Germany is not alone in opaque[10] statistics. The lobby group Plastics Recyclers Europe says that reported recycling rates across European countries don't reflect how much material is actually recovered.

choice of words: ________________

reality: ________________

[1] **to hail** to praise – [2] **dire** very serious or extreme – [3] **pastime** hobby – [4] **to spin a tale** to make up a story either to entertain or deceive (*täuschen*) sb. – [5] **unparalleled** better or greater than any other – [6] **to retain** (*fml.*) to keep or continue to have sth. – [7] **to generate** to bring into being, to cause – [8] **whopping** (*infml.*) much bigger than usual – [9] **deceptive** *trügerisch* – [10] **opaque** (*fml.*) difficult to understand

"The numbers are based on the amount of plastic waste collected rather than the amount of plastics finally recycled," Antonino Furfari, managing director of the lobby group, told DW.
Furfari says that the net recycling rate of countries with high reported numbers – including Germany, Lithuania and Slovenia – are actually much lower, for several reasons.
First of all, a lot of the waste that ends up in sorting facilities has been wrongly collected. In big cities in Germany, up to 50 percent of general rubbish ends up in the yellow bins designated for plastic, including packaging waste that needs to be separated from the valuable plastics.
Secondly, plastic packaging is often made from a variety of polymer[11] types. For example, meat packaging includes several protective layers to avoid discoloration of the contents, although only single-variety[12] plastics can be recycled. [...]
All of the "rejected" waste is either sent to landfills, where it sits for centuries, or to incineration sites[13] where it gets burned for heat or energy generation. Yet, this is counted as "recycled."

Downcycling

Another often-forgotten fact about recycling is that the recovered material degrades[14] in quality. Recycled plastic packaging can therefore not simply be used to produce new packaging material.
Recycled plastic bags, sandwich wrappers and juice bottles are typically turned into flower pots, coat hangers and other products that don't require high-quality material, such as that associated with food. Experts call this "downcycling."
In order to produce new food packaging, the industry needs to add new material – namely crude oil[15] – "which unnecessarily uses loads of resources and harms our environment," says Sommer. "We only have 'real' recycling with reusable bottles that are collected [from consumers with help of a deposit system] via supermarkets," he adds. Bottles made of polyethylene terephthalate – or PET – can be cleaned and refilled 25 times before they get recycled. Glass bottles can see 50 uses or more before they need to be recycled.
Germany does have the biggest collection system for reusable PET and glass bottles worldwide. "That's something we can be proud of," says Sommer, adding that an ongoing trend, however, is moving toward single-use bottles instead.

Plastic is for eternity

Plastic is cheap, robust and lightweight. It has transformed the way we consume – and in short, made our modern lifestyle possible.
Plastic is literally forever – it never actually biodegrades, only breaks down into ever-smaller pieces.
Packaging based on synthetic polymers has allowed supermarkets to offer a wider range of fresh produce that stays fresh longer. Computers, toothbrushes and synthetic clothing contain plastic.
Modern medicine has also greatly benefited from the disposable plastic syringe[16].
But our dependence on plastic is problematic. Microplastic has been found in Antarctica and the Arctic, not to mention tap water[17] worldwide.

euphemism: ________

real recycling: ________

plastic: ________

[11] **polymer** a chemical compound made by combining molecules – [12] **single-variety** *sortenrein* – [13] **incineration site** *Verbrennungsanlage* – [14] **to degrade** to spoil or destroy the quality of sth. – [15] **crude oil** *Rohöl* – [16] **syringe** [sɪˈrɪndʒ] *Spritze* – [17] **tap water** *Leitungswasser*

A study from 2016 has warned that unless the world takes drastic action to recycle, there will be more plastic than fish in the world's oceans by 2050.
Since mass production began in the 1950s, we've produced 8.3 billion metric tons of the material – and demand continues to grow.
In Europe, the amount of plastic waste has increased 13 percent in the last 10 years, mirroring a worldwide trend. […]

https://www.dw.com/en/plastic-waste-and-the-recycling-myth/a-45746469, 12 October 2018 [03.04.2021]

1 **Recycling plastic packaging**

Share of plastic packaging waste recycled

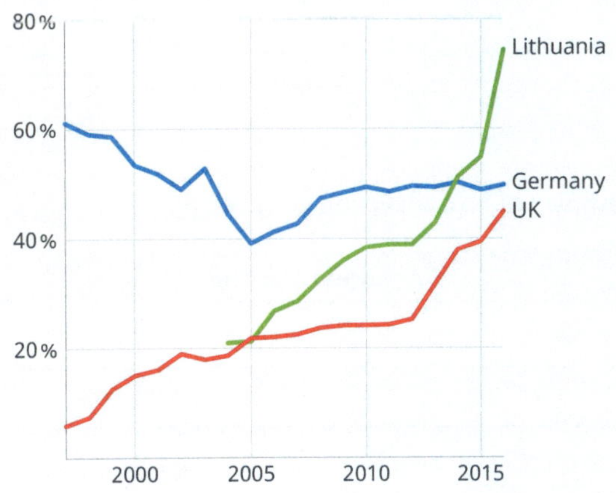

Source: Eurostat (env_waspac) © DW

Tips on vocab

1 a significant rise in/increase of … ■ an ongoing trend on a high/low level … ■ to reveal a striking difference in … ■ to stay on a … level …

Tips on vocab

2 a juxtaposition of different data ■ the most … the least … ■ to compare by … ■ a majority of/minority of … ■ to be wasted …

2 **Plastic: Wasted or recovered?**

Share of plastic packaging waste that is
■ Not recovered (e.g. ends up in landfills)
■ Recycled (e.g. materials reused)
■ Otherwise recovered (e.g. incinerated for energy)

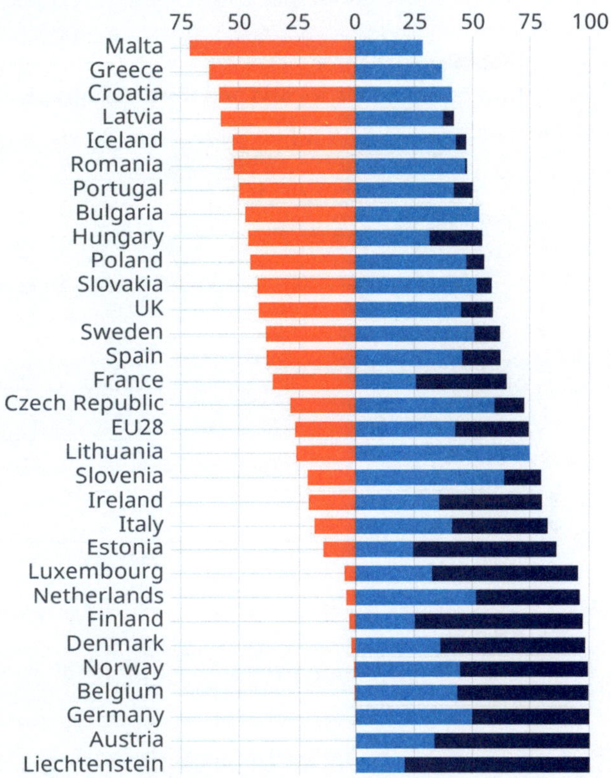

Source: Eurostat (env_waspac), latest available data for each country (2015 or 2016) © DW

COMPREHENSION

Before analysing the text at hand, read the article and clarify unknown words and phrases. Take notes in the margin and highlight or underline relevant aspects in the text using different colours for your notes and remarks (cf. box on p. 36).

ANALYSIS

Analyse the article and explain
a) the difference between the "recycling myth" and reality,
b) the alarming consequences that result from ignoring reality.

Step 1:

Take a closer look at the **first paragraph** and take notes on the German model of recycling and how it is applauded internationally.

measures taken	description by the author
• *different bins for different waste*	→ *national pastime*
• *deposit of plastic/glass bottles*	→ *pride*
• *the green dot*	→ *children's books*
•	→
•	→
•	→
•	→

Step 2:

Now, examine the **second** and **third paragraph** and find examples of how recycling goes wrong.

collecting	downcycling
•	•
•	•
•	•
•	•
•	•
•	•
•	•

Step 3:

Examine and compare the author's choice of words in the **fourth paragraph** when she describes the "qualities" of plastic.

☺	☹
• *cheap, robust …*	• *dependence …*
•	•
•	•
•	•
•	•
•	•
•	•

Step 4:
Analyse the line graph and the bar chart on p. 39 and explain:

- the trends of recycling plastic packaging in Lithuania, Germany, and the UK between 2000 and 2015

- the development of recovering plastic waste in countries of the European Union

- the overall trend that can be observed

Step 5:
Finally, write a coherent analysis of the article that considers and includes the statistics as well. Write about 250 – 300 words in which you

- examine Germany's position as a "recycling champion",
- contrast the numbers given in official statistics and reality,
- explain the dual character of plastics, i. e. its benefits and burdens.

Tip: Do not forget to prove the accuracy of your work by giving evidence from the text (quotes, lines).

Tips on vocab

- In the course of time …
- On the one hand … on the other hand …
- At the beginning … finally/lately …
- The numbers/data reveal that …
- The figures/statistics show an increase in …
- There has been an underestimation/ignorance of …

Prepare for ... Analysis of a (Political) Speech

Political speeches are usually intended to be listened to rather than to be read (only). However, often only a close reading (and analysis) enables you to literally "read between the lines" and get a deeper understanding of underlying messages and the implied meanings of certain formulations. In general, the purpose of most political speeches is to influence and appeal to the listener or reader by using a wide variety of structural and rhetorical devices.

Before analysing

- Read the speech at least two times and make sure that you have understood everything correctly.
- Look up specific words or phrases used and references made by the speaker to get a deeper understanding of the background and the topics mentioned.

While analysing

- Use of the **4-step method**:
  1) **identify the (structural, rhetorical, stylistic)** device in the text,
  2) **use the correct technical term** for the device,
  3) **write the line number(s)** where you found the device in the text,
  4) take notes on the possible **function of the device** and the **intended effect**.
- Use different colours for your labellings and notes in the margin of the text to get a better overview of the various devices employed in the speech.
- As you are expected to explain the function, effect or message of certain devices in particular and the speech in general, pay attention to your formulations (see Info box p. 47).
- Use the simple present as the predominant tense for your analysis to give your text a matter-of-fact style.

Colours used for markings and labellings in the texts:

- content → **blue**
- stylistic devices → **red**
- narrative/structural devices → **orange**
- allusions/symbols/references → **green**

Practise …
Analysing Rhetorical Devices in a Political Speech

Nkosilathi Nyathi

UNICEF Climate Advocate Speech on Climate Change and SDGs

Nkosilathi Nyathi (*2003) is a Zimbabwean environmental activist who has been appointed UNICEF Youth Climate Ambassador for Zimbabwe in 2015, 2020 and beyond.
In 2019, the area of Victoria Falls, Zimbabwe, suffered from the worst drought in a century, and about 7.7 million Zimbabwean people now live at the risk of hunger.
In the speech at hand, delivered at the African Regional Forum on Sustainable Development at Victoria Falls on 25 February 2020, Nyathi demanded of world leaders that they include young people and urged them to tackle climate change and reach the 2030 Sustainable Development Goals (SDGs).

introduction: ______ ______

Good Morning. My name is Nkosilathi Nyathi, and I am a UNICEF-Climate Youth Ambassador and a proud Zimbabwean and African youth under the Zimbabwe Youth Council.
Welcome to Victoria Falls. My home. It is also home to the magnificent Victoria Falls or in our local Lozi language, Mosi-oa-tunya which means the 'Smoke that Thunders'.

device: ______ ______

I grew up just a few minutes from where we are today. In Chinotimba township. And while I grew up in poverty, with everybody struggling all around me, I noticed something that affected the poverty of my community, of my family and friends, just as much as all the economic and social problems and the political issues we face in my country.

______ ______ ______

It was the environment! Our natural world around us, our atmosphere and our biodiversity[1].
We are experiencing the worst drought[2], right here in my backyard, in 100 years. I live it. My family lives it. Farmers have had little harvest for years now. When it doesn't rain we suffer. And now when it does rain, it floods and we suffer.

device: ______ ______

Two weeks ago, about one hundred kilometres down the Zambezi river the town of Binga was left devastated after many homes and livelihoods were washed away by floods.
We all know about the devastating impact of Cyclone Idai that hit Mozambique, Malawi and Zimbabwe last year turning the lives of 1 million children upside down.
Friends, leaders …
Climate Change is now our reality. It is causing these extreme weather events to be more frequent and more severe. The plagues of locusts[3] that are decimating[4] Eastern Africa – many of your countries – are made worse through climatic impacts such as drought and floods.

______ ______ ______

Since I was 10, I have been passionate about this.

[1] **biodiversity** [ˌbaɪəʊdaɪˈvɜːsəti] the variety of plants and animals that exist in a particular area – [2] **drought** [draʊt] a long period of little or no rain – [3] **locust** *Heuschrecke* – [4] **to decimate** to reduce sth. severely

device:

reference:

choice of words:

device:

I am proud that I have been part of environmental clubs since grade 5.
I am currently the vice president of the environmental club at my school – Inyathi high school.
In December last year I embarked on the biggest adventure of my life. I had the honour of speaking at the COP[5] 25 in Madrid. I experienced and was involved in the debates, the meetings and the negotiations to figure out how we can lower our emissions and adapt to climate change. It opened my eyes to the huge efforts going on at the global scale.
But what struck[6] me, as I nervously sat in that airplane for the first time, and I looked down at the parched[7] landscape of Zimbabwe and Southern Africa with farmland laying bare, the rivers and dams drying up.
I thought to myself that there millions of children and young people down there dealing with these harsh environments, food shortages and failing social conditions on the ground. They … We are the future.
We are here to talk about Sustainable[8] Development. But we need to recognise that the environment and climate change form the foundation of all the SDGs.
If we fail to achieve the goals related to Clean Water and Sanitation, Climate Action, Life Below Water, and Life on Land, the world will fail to achieve all the other remaining goals.
The eradication[9] of poverty, zero hunger, peace and justice, education, good health, just to name a few. These are the goals that affect my life every day!
Protecting the environment is one of the most important requirements for social justice and economic development … and ensuring the rights of children all around the world.
In Spain I called on the leaders at the COP to work extra hard to solve the climate and biodiversity emergency.
I also made a plea[10] to involve us – the voices and opinions of children and young people – in creating the policies and making decisions about the climate and environment, which in the end will impact us and our children in the future.
I am happy that in Zimbabwe, the government involved young people the production of the country's climate policy document. But please, can the plans now become actions!
We are here. We are smart. We are activists. We have solutions. Involve us!
Did you know that when I was 14, I invented a biogas stove[11] in my backyard? I learned that if we composted food scraps in a special container they would breakdown and provide natural gas that could be tapped[12] into a stove to cook on.
I built it. And it not only reuses our food and kitchen waste in a sustainable way, but it meant we don't need to rely on burning fossil fuels for energy. And in a place like Zimbabwe, where we have a terrible fuel and power crisis, this helped us survive.

[5] **COP** Conference of the Parties; UN Climate Change Conference – [6] **to strike** here: to make a big impression on sb. – [7] **parched** dried out because of too much heat and not enough rain – [8] **sustainable** *nachhaltig* – [9] **eradication** the process of getting rid of sth. or destroying sth. – [10] **plea** *Gesuch, Appell* – [11] **stove** a device that is used to heat and cook food – [12] **to tap sth.** *etw. anzapfen*

So friends and leaders …
As I speak to you here today on this stage, with my President beside me, other important leaders and decision makers, down here on the ground in Victoria Falls, in my backyard. I make a bigger plea to you … A demand. Please take all the things we talk about and debate this week and put it into action … Young people have already started putting their words into practice through the various forums on Youth SDGs. Go back to Harare, to Nairobi, to Pretoria, to Geneva to New York[13] and Act!
But in doing so, call on your young people … the student leaders, the activists, the science enthusiasts, the video gamers, the young sports stars and bring them into the rooms when you are planning your actions and policies. Listen to their views and ideas!
Because …
'Nothing for us, without us, is for us'
I hope you enjoy your stay in my hometown and that for generations to come Mosi-oa-tunya's smoke continues to thunder!

Thank you

https://www.unicef.org/zimbabwe/stories/unicef-climate-advocate-speech-climate-change-and-sdgs, 27 February 2020 [03.04.2021]

device: ____________________

device: ____________________

COMPREHENSION

While reading the speech
- subdivide the speech into thematic units,
- take notes in the text margin on problems Nyathi mentions,
- underline or highlight most relevant information in the text using different colours (cf. box on p. 42).

ANALYSIS

Examine and analyse the formal, stylistic, and rhetorical devices employed in the speech and relate their function and effect to the intended message of Nyathi's speech.

Tip: In order to make sure that you have understood the complex task correctly, highlight and/or underline the relevant key words (e. g. *Operatoren*, verbs, nouns).

Step 1:
The grid below helps you to focus on the most relevant devices, which are listed in the left column. Identify these devices in the speech and take notes in the centre column of the grid.

Tip: Do not forget to note down the line(s) where you found the device.

devices	example from text, line(s)	function/effect
formal devices		
• **paragraphs**	• ____________	____________

[13] **Harare, Nairobi, Pretoria, Geneva, New York** reference to cities where COP climate change conferences were held in the past

devices	example from text, line(s)	function/effect
• sentence structure	• ____	____
• references	• ____	____
stylistic devices		
• word fields	• ____	____
• key words and phrases	• ____	____
• repetitions	• ____	____
rhetorical devices		
• parallelism	• ____	____

devices	example from text, line(s)	function/effect
• climax	•	
• grammatical persons	•	
• grammatical tenses	•	
Intention/message of the speech:		

Step 2:
After completing your notes in the grid, think about the (intended) function and effect of the devices and take notes in the right column.

Info

Here is a short overview of the function and effect certain devices create:

paragraphs
→ structure the text into thematic units; make the text easier to read and understand

sentence structure
→ short sentences and ellipsis increase the speed of a spoken text, can make it sound more aggressive
→ long sentences slow down the speed

word fields
→ create a certain mood or atmosphere

key words/phrases
→ attract particular attention; stay in the readers' or listeners' mind

repetition
→ emphasis on specific aspects or problems

parallelism/anaphora
→ focus on important aspects by repeating them

enumeration/climax
→ a development or trend is emphasized or dramatized

grammatical persons
→ means of inclusion and solidarity (we, our, us) or exclusion (I – you; we – they)

grammatical tenses
→ indirect references to past … present … future events

Step 3:
Identify the message of the speech by checking and using your notes concerning the function and effect of certain devices.

Tip: Of course, the predominant intention of most political speeches is to influence and appeal to the listeners. However, here your task is to be more precise and explain the function of the speech and its devices in detail.

Tips on vocab

- The speaker expresses doubts/questions …
- The first/second … part runs from line … to line …
- The choice of words gives the speech a character …
- The phrase suggests …
- The speaker establishes a relationship between … by …
- The speaker's claims are …
- He supports his claim with …

Tips on vocab

The speaker …
- … defends his party's/government's objectives …
- … points out his own/his party's merits …
- … blames others for …
- … appeals to emotions rather than reason …
- … attacks his opponent …
- … identifies with the audience by …
- … wants the listeners to adopt his view on …
- … aims to get the listeners to act/to take action …
- … uses techniques of persuasion …
- … uses emotive language, e. g. …
- … uses stereotypes, e. g. …
- … does not state clearly/precisely …
- … frequently uses …
- … employs an elaborated/informal … choice of words …
- … intends to …

Step 4:
As a political speech is an argumentative text, it is important to have a close look at the speaker's train of thought and line of argument in order to better understand the structure of the speech. Following the paragraphs and/or topical order of the text, filter out the essential aspects and arrange your findings in a flow chart that illustrates the logical order of the argumentation.

Example:

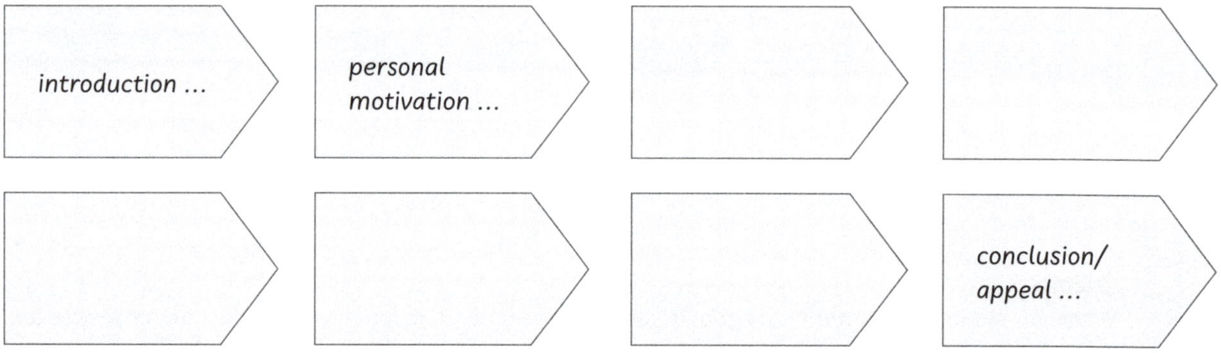

Step 5:
In his speech, Nyathi repeatedly refers to the SDGs, the Sustainable Development Goals set up and published by UNICEF years ago. Take a look at the infographic on page 49 and identify
- the social, humanitarian, economic, political and environmental focus each goal takes,
- the ranking of the different goals.

Which of these goals does Nyathi mention or refer to in his speech? And why?

Step 6:
Finally, using your findings and notes from the flow cart and the grid, write an analysis of the speech of about 350 words. Use the "Tips on vocab" boxes for further help and to make your text flow better.

Example:
Nkosilathi Nyathi opens his speech given at … on …, by introducing himself and referring to himself as an inhabitant of … and …

Tips on vocab

adding information and ■ as well as ■ additionally ■ moreover	**sequencing** firstly ■ secondly ■ then ■ next ■ following ■ meanwhile ■ wafterwards ■ finally ■ so far	**comparing** equally ■ like ■ in the same way ■ compared with ■ equally ■ as with ■ likewise ■ similarly
contrasting although ■ whereas ■ otherwise ■ but ■ instead of ■ alternatively ■ in spite of ■ even if	**exception** except (for) ■ unless ■ if ■ whether	**cause & effect** as a result ■ therefore ■ thus ■ because
adding an idea provided that ■ apart from ■ if ■ however ■ furthermore ■ in addition to ■ as well as	**emphasizing** significantly ■ especially ■ in particular ■ above all ■ more important ■ especially ■ above all ■ in particular ■ indeed	**giving examples** for example ■ such as ■ namely ■ in the case of ■ for instance
arguing therefore ■ thus ■ since ■ because ■ as a result	**persuading** surely ■ obviously ■ certainly ■ of course ■ naturally	**opinion/analysis** one might infer/say/conclude ■ it would seem that …
summing up in summary ■ in brief ■ finally ■ on the whole ■ in the end ■ in all		

Prepare for ... Analysis of a Cartoon

A **cartoon** is a comic or satirical drawing that aims at (humorously) criticizing current political or social events. Most cartoons consist of a **pictorial part** (one or more drawings) and a **textual part** (a speech balloon, comment or caption (= short title)).

"Is the homework gluten free?"

Before analysing

- Reflect on the topic or event the cartoon focuses on and do further research on it to gain some **background knowledge**.
- **Describe the cartoon** and its elements in detail:
  - Which elements are placed in the centre (= most relevant), which are in the background, etc.? Which visual elements and symbols (e. g. colour, contrast, etc.) and visual symbols are employed?
  - What is the political, historical or social background of the cartoon?
- **Use a specific structure** for the description of the cartoon, e. g.
  - the "from the inside to the outside" method (i. e. from general aspects to details)
  - the "from the foreground to the background" method (= "going into the picture")

While analysing

- **Label the various elements** of the cartoon, using different colours (cf. box below) and take notes on relevant aspects.
- Consider the **symbolic or figurative level** of the various elements of the cartoon:
  - What do the symbols used stand for or allude to?
  - Which tools are used to achieve a certain effect or convey an intended message (e. g. irony, parody, allusion/reference, hyperbole/exaggeration, black humour, etc.)?
- Determine the **message** of the cartoon.

Colours used for markings and labellings in the texts:

- content → blue
- stylistic devices → red
- narrative/structural devices → orange
- allusions/symbols/references → green

Practise ... Identifying and Explaining Details and Symbols in a Cartoon

Social media have become the most important communication platform for many people. Particularly for teenagers it is often their major tool of communicating with friends.
However, there are two sides of the coin as bullying people virtually has become a sad reality as well. Teenagers and even children are often harassed, exposed and humiliated publicly through hate-mails, embarrassing photos or video clips.
The two cartoons on the following pages deal with various forms of cyberbullying. You can either work with both or just choose one of them to practise your cartoon analysis skills.

Thomas Plaßmann

Cyberbullying

bullies: ____________________

eye-catcher/
visual symbol: ____________________

bullies: ____________________

1

Thomas Plaßmann, 02 December 2020

source: ____________________

victim: ____________________

Tips on vocab

an oversized fist/thumb ■ to clomp sb. (virtually) into the ground ■ remotely controlled fist ■ to have mean facial expressions ■ to struggle desperately ■ bulging eyes

Zach

Virtually Smacked

eye-catcher/visual symbol: ______________________

reference: ______________________

tool: ______________________

Zach, 19 October 2020, on: https://toonpool.com

source: ______________________

victim: ______________________

Tips on vocab

a mechanical fist on a spring ■ a Jack-in-the-box (toy) ■ to smash sb.'s face ■ to hit out a tooth ■ to hurt/injure sb. severely ■ an alienated company logo in the shape of a devil

COMPREHENSION

Before analysing the cartoons, describe the various elements in detail, using the tips and information given on page 50 as well as the Tips on vocab boxes below the cartoons.

Tip: Use the present progressive as the predominant tense for your description and do not forget to write an introductory sentence that includes the w-questions (who – what – where – when – why?).

ANALYSIS

Examine the deeper meaning and message of the cartoon(s):

a) Explain what in particular makes cyberbullying so dangerous and "effective".

b) Explain the political and societal implications Zach refers to and criticizes in the cartoon "Virtually Smacked".

Step 1:
Complete the labellings in the margin of the cartoon(s) and add further notes concerning references and/or allusions made.

Step 2:
Fill in the grid below and
a) name the various elements and
b) take notes on the references and allusions made.

Cartoon no. 1:

pictorial element	reference/allusion	function
the bullies	• *using virtual violence* •	→ *no direct contact/shows anonymity*
the victim	• *pressed into the ground* •	→
the fist/thumb	• *extended arm/fist* •	→

Cartoon no. 2:

pictorial element	reference/allusion	function
the smartphone	• *alienated Apple logo* •	→
the fist	• *like a "Jack-in-the-box" (= children's toy)* •	→
the victim/user	• •	→

Step 3:
Determine the effect and function of the visual elements of the cartoon(s).

Tip: Pay attention to changes and alienations made to well-known icons, symbols and logos and think about the intended message.

Step 4:
Cross-check your findings and notes and write a coherent analysis of your chosen cartoon of about 300 words.

Tip: Be careful to use the simple present as the predominant tense for your analysis.

Tips on vocab

The cartoonist ...
- visualizes/illustrates a current problem ...
- puts emphasis on showing ...
- presents reality in an exaggerated way ...
- puts an everyday situation to the extreme ...
- implies the view that ...
- aims at presenting/revealing ...

The cartoon ...
- criticizes the global IT companies by ...
- presents visual symbols ...
- puts ... in focus ...
- reveals the problem of ...
- exposes the hidden danger of ...

Prepare for ... Preparing and Conducting a Presentation

Preparing a presentation

"You should know I like sales presentations the way I like my soft boiled eggs: three minutes and you're done."

- **Do research** on the topic you want to present, but don't overdo it – have a clear focus on what you want to get across.
- **Select the most relevant points** and don't overload the audience.
- Use the **postcard technique**:
  a) Break your presentation into thematic sections or units.
  b) Give each section or unit a heading.
  c) Write one heading and a few easily-read prompt words (notes) on each postcard.
  d) Number the postcards in the order that you want to present these points.
- If possible, **provide audio-visual aids** (e.g. a PowerPoint, transparencies, CD, large poster, etc.) and a handout for each person.

Giving a presentation

- Greet the audience and introduce yourself.
- Speak more slowly and loudly than usual.
- Look up and make eye contact.
- At the beginning, briefly outline your topic.
- Explain difficult words or technical terms to your audience.
- At the end, thank your audience and ask them if there are any questions they want to ask.

Practise ... Presenting a (Controversial) Topic

Since the 19th century, sociologists have been trying to distinguish, categorize and characterize various generations of the Western world.
So far, they have identified the generational cohorts (*Geburtsjahrgang*) from the "Lost Generation" (born 1880 – 1900) up to "Generation Alpha" (born 2010 – 2025).

What Is the Generation Gap?

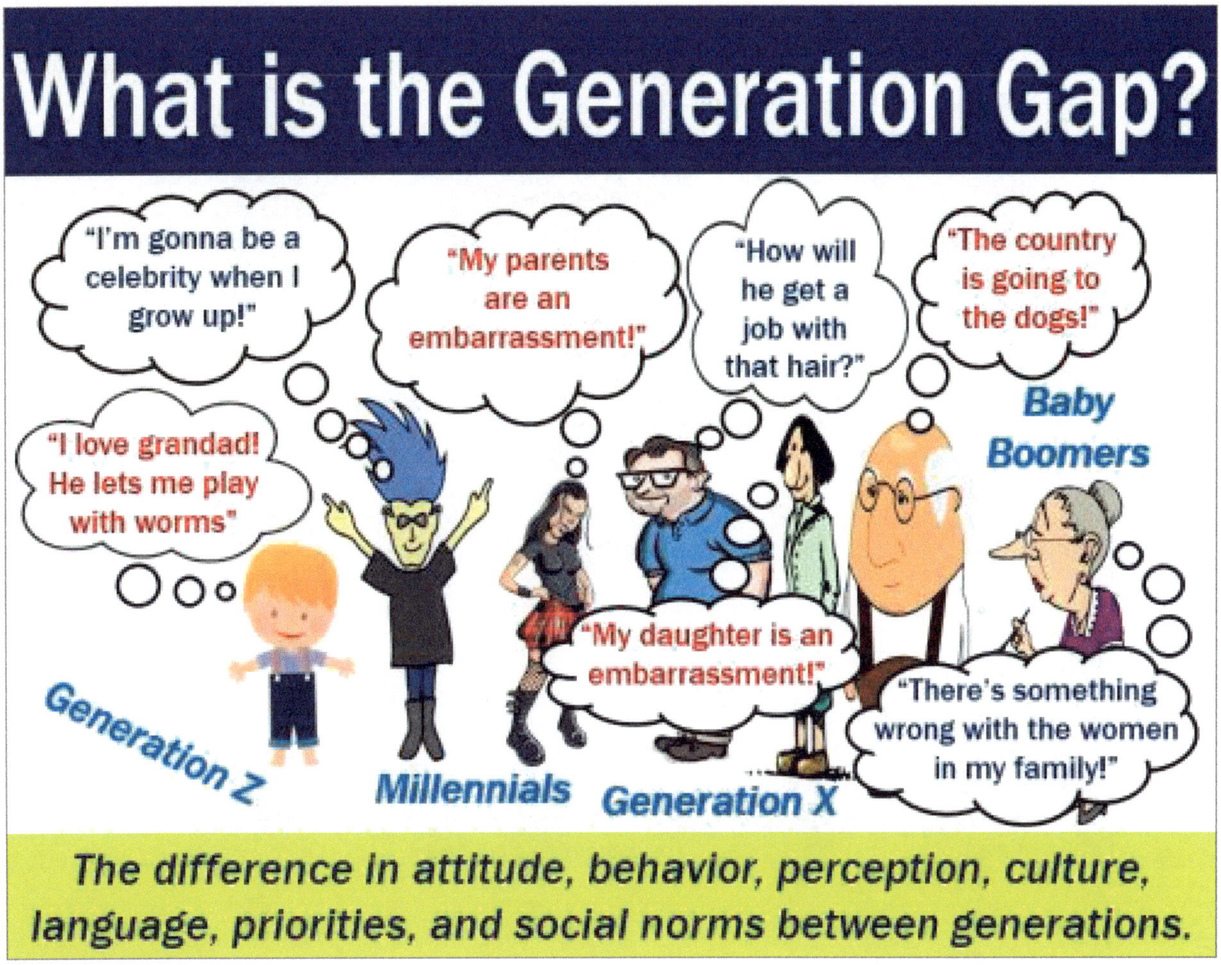

Market Business News, 2022

Tips on vocab

a toddler ■ a freak with dyed (blue) hair wearing stylish sunglasses ■ a girl dressed as a punk (pleated tartan skirt, fishnet stockings, combat boots) ■ a concerned father ■ an embarrassed mother ■ a frustrated senior/grandfather (bald, wearing rimmed glasses, pants with suspenders) ■ a concerned grandmother (wearing rimmed glasses, grey hair, hair in a bun, having an indignant/annoyed facial expression)

COMMUNICATION

Prepare a presentation in which you
a) give an overview of the different generational cohorts so far,
b) point out the characteristics of each generation,
c) describe generational gaps and possible causes of and reason for them.

Step 1:
Study the infographic on the previous page and explain what the expressions and speech bubbles reveal about the attitude of the respective generation.

Step 2:
Explain the definition of the term "generation gap" and try to find examples for each of the categories depicted in the infographic. Take notes in the grid below.

generation	attitude/behaviour	perception/priorities/ social norms	culture	language
Baby Boomers	• *critical* • *negative* • •			
Generation X		• *getting a job*		
Millennials		• *becoming a celebrity*		
Generation Z				

Step 3:
Do further research on the various generations in Western society and get further information about their characteristics. Take notes on your findings and complete the grid.

Step 4:
Find out about the historical, societal and economic background of each generation and how it has influenced them.

Step 5:
On the basis of your research results, now focus on the central aspect of your presentation, i. e.:
What are the striking generational differences and which consequences does this have with regard to societal gaps or controversies?

Step 6:
Finally, prepare your postcards and/or visual aids and give your presentation. The Tips on vocab box below gives you some help for your formulations.

Tips on vocab

to study/examine sth. ■ to do a careful study of … ■ to distinguish between … ■ to draw a difference between ■ to establish a relationship between … and … ■ to relate … with/to … ■ to be in contact to … ■ to show the consequences of … ■ with results from … ■ this leads to … ■ to take an idealistic/realistic/critical view of …

Prepare for … Conducting an Interview

Although the interviewer's job generally is to show an interest in the interviewee and his/her situation and to elicit (*entlocken*) information from him/her, the interviewer's foremost job is to be **neutral, unemotional and unbiased**.

Before interviewing

- **Get informed** about the person you are about to interview, such as his/her personal or professional background.
- **Pre-formulate** questions on important or interesting aspects but stay open to the interviewee's focus and priorities on a certain matter he/she considers to be important.

While interviewing

- Introduce yourself to the interviewee and mention the topic of or reason for the interview.
- Ask questions that are **precise and well-structured**.
- Listen and react to the interviewee, e. g. ask follow-up questions.
- Ask questions that are precise and respectful.
- End the interview by summarizing the result of the discussion or talk and thanking the participant(s).

Info

1) **yes-no question** → Do you love dancing?
2) **open question** → What actually made you start dancing? What are your further plans?
3) **question after statement** → You have gained international attention on YouTube … What was your first reaction?
4) **question referring back** → Let's get back to your initial statement … What made you think …?
5) **confrontational question** → What do you respond to people who say dancing is just for girls?
6) **indirectly expressed question** → Well, I thought you might be interested in giving us an overview of …

Colours used for markings and labellings in the texts:

- content → blue
- stylistic devices → red
- narrative/structural devices → orange
- allusions/symbols/references → green

Practise ... Interviewing a Teenager on a Controversial Topic

Emmanuel Akinwotu

Poise[1] and Prestige: Viral[2] Clip Propels[3] Lagos Ballet Class to Global Stage

Life for many Nigerian children and teenagers is very difficult and full of deprivation (*Entbehrung*), especially when they live in the dilapidated, impoverished outskirts of Lagos, a big Nigerian harbour city. Because of this and his love for ballet, Daniel Ajala was inspired and motivated to found the Leap of Dance Academy in Ajangbadi, a small town near Lagos, where he teaches boys and girls ballet.

How Anthony Madu and his Leap[4] of Dance Academy classmates won over the world

Eleven-year-old Anthony Madu glides barefoot across an uneven concrete floor, summoning[5] his frame into seamless[6] twirls[7] and conjuring[8] pirouettes, his poise effortless as rain falls into puddles around him.

The 45-second video, shot in June outside the home of his ballet teacher in Ajangbadi, an isolated, end-of-the-road coastal town on the outskirts[9] of Lagos, was intended to help Anthony practise his form.

Anthony: ______ ______ ______

Instead, the clip – a quietly stunning triumph of will over modest means – went viral, setting off an epic[10], internet-era fairytale. Celebrity and commercial endorsements[11], prestigious scholarship offers and pledges[12] for funding have flooded in, transforming the lives of Anthony, his teacher Daniel Ajala and other children at the Leap of Dance Academy. Local perceptions[13] of the academy – which weren't always positive – have also been upended[14].

choice of words: ______ ______

"When you're doing ballet you can feel like you're in a different place," Anthony said on a recent morning at ballet class in the dim light of a school hall in Ajangbadi, as other students set up balancing frames[15] and pinned rainbow-coloured drapes[16] on the walls.

"When I first started it was really painful, my thighs[17], my legs, my arms. My 'back walk-over', I couldn't do it," he said, gently arching[18] his back into a curve to demonstrate, "but then it got easier, or I did certain things so it wasn't so painful."

______ ______ ______

The first day after the video was posted on Instagram, an amazed "Mr Daniel" showed the children how far it had reached. "It was really exciting and made me feel joyful," Anthony said. In the days that followed, their amazement only grew as global attention soared[19].

In August Anthony gained a full scholarship to an online summer programme at the prestigious Jacqueline Kennedy Onassis School of American Ballet. In January he begins a five-year scholarship programme in New York. Similar offers have been made for some of the academy's other children.

reference: ______ ______

[1] **poise** grace and balance – [2] **viral** becoming popular very quickly – [3] **to propel** [prəˈpel] to cause sth. to move forward – [4] **leap** jump – [5] **to summon** to call up sth. for a use – [6] **seamless** here: without interruption – [7] **twirl** *Drehung* – [8] **to conjure** to call up as if by magic – [9] **outskirts** *Stadtrand* – [10] **epic** *sagenhaft* – [11] **endorsement** support – [12] **pledge** *Zusage* – [13] **perception** *Wahrnehmung* – [14] **to upend** to change – [15] **balancing frame** *Ballettstange* – [16] **drapes** curtains – [17] **thigh** *Oberschenkel* – [18] **to arch** *wölben* – [19] **to soar** to rise very quickly to a high level

What began for Anthony and his classmates as an immersive[20] if demanding[21] leisure activity has spawned[22] lofty[23] dreams. "I want to become a professional dancer. I believe I can achieve it," he beamed[24]. The setting of the academy and its modest intentions reinforce the unlikely nature of its remarkable tale.

word field:

Ajangbadi sits off the battered[25] Lagos to Badagry expressway, towards Nigeria's western border with Benin. Gusts[26] from the coastline breeze through the wide open spaces of the sandy, broken roads. Many of the nearby expressways and side roads have buckled[27] under the weight of large trucks that take cargo from water and yogurt factories into the city, leaving Ajangbadi and other more affordable suburban towns like it feeling inaccessible[28] and isolated.

Some of the students clustered[29] around 40-year-old Mary Olawale, applying makeup and glitter on their faces. Olawale moved to Ajangbadi 10 years ago, and began as an assistant at the academy after enrolling her two children. For her children, the academy was an oasis.

Daniel Ajala:

"In 2018, I took my daughters here to learn, have something to do," she said. "But then I came and saw how he [Ajala] was inspiring them, giving them life tools. What he is doing for the children is incredible."

Ajala started teaching ballet at after-school clubs in inner-city Lagos eight years ago, while studying business administration at university. He said he could have made money setting up a studio in more affluent pockets of the city, capitalising on a well-established and growing demand for ballet. "But I thought about it and I wanted to establish it here, in this neighbourhood, this is where it would matter more," he said.

He taught ballet to himself at home, watching videos on YouTube, and through social media, joining international dance networks. After leaving university, he unnerved his parents when he told them that he was pursuing[30] dance teaching over a more typical profession. "I knew this was my calling, so I had no doubts at all," he said.

word field:

He envisioned the academy as a place where children could gain a greater sense of what they could be, not necessarily through dance. "I want them to have confidence in themselves and what they can aspire[31] to. It's about exposure[32]. We're looking at online references, learning, using a range of resources, I believe that is powerful."

reference:

reactions/ repercussions:

Outside the lessons, Ajala and the children have encountered[33] stiff[34] resistance in the community. At one point more than 30 children attended classes, but almost two-thirds were withdrawn by their parents. "People were saying 'ballet is demonic[35]', that it was corrupting[36] them, that parents shouldn't allow their kids to go," Ajala said. In particular, suspicions were stirred by the sight of boys wearing tights[37] and makeup and participating in what some saw as an effeminate[38] and western art form.

The school hall is also used by a local church, whose pastor began confronting Ajala when they crossed paths. "She would say: 'Boys shouldn't be wearing tights', 'the ballet is the reason why the church attendance is getting low' – things like that."

[20] **immersive** *vereinnahmend* – [21] **demanding** needing a lot of time, attention or energy – [22] **to spawn** to cause sth. new to grow suddenly – [23] **lofty** high – [24] **to beam** *leuchten* – [25] **battered** hurt by being hit – [26] **gust** a sudden strong wind – [27] **to buckle** here: *zusammenbrechen* – [28] **inaccessible** very difficult or impossible to reach – [29] **to cluster** to form a group – [30] **to pursue** *verfolgen* – [31] **to aspire to sth.** (*phr. v.*) to have a strong will to do sth. – [32] **exposure** *mediale Präsenz* – [33] **to encounter** to experience sth. unpleasant – [34] **stiff** firm or hard – [35] **demonic** wild and evil – [36] **to corrupt sb.** to make sb. become dishonest and immoral – [37] **tights** *Strumpfhosen* – [38] **effeminate** feminine

Warnings by church officials have had greater influence in this remote, cautious community, where the functions and protections of state structures are barely visible. Few people in the community regarded ballet as worthwhile, in contrast to more urban areas, where the cultural capital associated with the art form fuels[39] its appeal[40].

At one point, a friend advised Ajala to use the time he was investing in the academy to earn money. “I just thought about it seriously but I realised that this was what God wants me to do,” he said.

Since June, perceptions have gradually changed, and there is more of a sense locally of the opportunities the school can offer. The academy has a waiting list of 30 children, and another school where Ajala used to hold classes, which had said it could no longer accommodate[41] him, is “begging for us to come back”.

allusion:

new perceptions:

Before the coronavirus pandemic Ajala held classes three times a week in a school hall. When schools closed he moved lessons to his home, where they took place almost daily. The children trained in bare feet, to preserve their ballet shoes from tearing[42] on his concrete floor.

Every week brings new visitors, some with cameras and filming equipment. The children’s poses are still poised[43] and carefree, but the children themselves are more practised, more at ease[44] in limelight[45].

“We could have never expected that any of this would happen, to this degree,” Ajala said. “It’s incredible and goes to show that for the students anything they set their mind to is possible.”

https://www.theguardian.com/stage/2020/sep/04/poise-and-prestige-the-lagos-ballet-class-propelled-onto-global-stage, 4 September 2020 [02.04.2021]

Anthony and classmates practising. ‘When you’re doing ballet you can feel like you’re in a different place.’ Photo: Manny Jefferson, 4 September 2020, in: The Guardian

COMPREHENSION

Read the article from the British newspaper *The Guardian* closely and take notes in the margin.

- Underline and/or highlight relevant information.
- Pay attention to the specific choice of words in connection with certain aspects.
- Make a list of the relevant people mentioned in the article for your interview later on.

[39] **to fuel** to provide power to sth. – [40] **appeal** the quality in sb. that makes him/her attractive or interesting – [41] **to accommodate** to provide with a room or rooms – [42] **to tear (tore, torn)** [teər] to pull apart – [43] **poised** full of grace and balance – [44] **at ease** relaxed – [45] **limelight** public attention and interest

COMMUNICATION

You are a journalist of an international youth magazine and want to get more information about the Leap of Dance Academy and their story of success. Conduct an interview with
a) its founder, Daniel Ajala,
b) Anthony Madu about his dreams and hopes,
c) the pastor of the neighbouring church,
d) parents of Ajala's ballet students.

WES-121502-010

Step 1: To prepare for the interview, watch the video clip provided on the webcode which presents Anthony Madu and Daniel Ajala's Leap of Dance Academy and get an impression of their project.

Step 2: Do further research on the Leap of Dance Academy to back up your interview questions.

Step 3: With regard to your assignment, collect and sort the information you have gained about the topic, using the grid below.

Daniel Ajala	Anthony Madu	the pastor	parents

Step 4: Now, formulate your questions.

Tip: Use the tips given in the Info box on p. 58 on how to best formulate and vary the style of your questions.

Examples:
- *Mr. Ajala, how do you feel when you think about your students?*
- *Mr. Ajala, can you tell our readers why you founded the Leap of Dance Academy?*
- *Leap of Dance, what an interesting name. How did you get the idea …?*
- *Anthony, what is your life like in New York?*

Step 5: After formulating a collection of questions, put yourself in the position of the interviewee and think about possible answers that reflect the person's situation and position.

Tip: In order to make the interview more realistic you should employ linguistic devices and communicative strategies such as
- "fillers": *Well …; Actually …; Let's see …; Now let me think …; I see what you mean …*
- feedback phrases to emphasize that you are listening closely
- friendly comments to create a conciliatory atmosphere
- turn-taking phrases to prompt the other person to speak: *I agree with what say, but let me ask you …*
- avoiding judgemental comments
- expressing yourself indirectly by using conditional forms
- making a pause after a statement
- question tags: *You have put so much energy into the project, haven't you?*
- making suggestions

Basics for Your Writing

1. Structuring and outlining ideas

- Follow the **introduction – main part – conclusion** pattern.
- Sort and structure ideas and organize your thoughts before writing, e.g. by using a mind map or a flow chart.
- Collect ideas, thoughts, reasons and examples and arrange them according to how they fit together; leave out everything out that does not seem logical, relevant or effective and does not precisely match your task or the purpose of the text.
- Collect arguments, reasons and make clear whether you are arguing for or against a particular issue.
- Follow the pattern "one paragraph – one main idea" and stay focused. Begin each paragraph with a new line.

2. A good beginning and ending

- The beginning of a good writing should grab the reader's attention and evoke his/her interest.
- The beginning introduces the topic or problem and should give an overview of it (e. g. answer the w-questions who – where – when – what – why?).
- Depending on your focus, the beginning can be provocative (e. g. a question, concise statement or quotation) or informative (giving an overview of the topic and its background).
- The ending should shortly summarize the relevant aspects and information given, or conclude with a final statement that sums up your or the author's point of view.

3. Simplicity | brevity | conciseness

- A good text is kept to the essentials. Therefore avoid filler words and getting lost in the details.
- Avoid over-explaining everything; if information is not essential to help understand your message, leave it out.
- Vary the length of your sentences to give your writing a nice flow but avoid wordy explanations. Sentences of 10 – 20 words should do.
- Participle constructions help to shorten sentences but don't overdo it – too many participle constructions make your text sound very formal and stiff.
- Avoid repetition by paraphrasing words and varying the beginning of the sentences (cf. vocab box in Skill 7, p. 49)

4. Avoiding clichés and meaningless padding

- Eliminate unclear thoughts and banal generalizations.
- Keep your language simple and direct and leave out empty words and phrases.
- Eliminate or reduce unnecessary filler words and phrases (e. g. daily ~~at all times~~, ~~each and every~~, in order, very, really, basically, essentially, rather, quite, extremely, simply, pretty, just, as a matter of fact, during ~~the course of~~, now ~~at this point in time~~).

5. Reading out loud

- Reading your writing aloud can help to check whether it flows or sounds choppy and clipped. If it sounds too monotonous, add a few longer sentences.

6. Editing | proof-reading | revising

- Finally, cross-check your writing to make necessary additions and alterations and to shorten or eliminate passages that are repetitive or not precise enough.

Prepare for ... Creative Writing

Although the assignment to continue a fictional text requires creativity, you are not absolutely free in what you are going to write. Instead, your writing should be based on the text you are given and you should employ its characteristic features.

Before writing

- **Identify the characteristic features** of the literary genre and the type of text you are required to work with creatively, e. g.

narrative texts		dramatized texts		film script
novel	**short story**	**classical drama**	**modern play**	**screenplay**
• narrator/narrative perspective • character(s) • panoramic/scenic presentation • main/sub-plot stream of consciousness • interior monologue • development of action/plot • disruptions/lapses in time/foreshadowing/flashback, etc. • spoken/everyday English, informal English	• immediate beginning • open ending • exceptional incident in everyday life • spoken English	• protagonist/ • antagonist/hero • dialogue/monologue/soliloquy • stage directions • acts/scenes • spoken English • development of a conflict • often linear development • happy/tragic ending/resolution	• everyday character(s) • internal conflict • current topics, e. g. society, politics, crisis, war, etc. • stage directions • disruptions/lapses in time • spoken English	• slug lines • dialogue/monologue • action • focus on visual aspects • technical directions (props, music, camera operations) • spoken English

- **Be prepared** to employ (some of) these characteristics in your text.
- There can be different creative writing tasks, e. g.
  - continue a chapter from a novel or from a scene of a play,
  - change the narrative perspective and time, e.g. switch to a different time, from first-person narrator to third-person (omniscient), etc.,
  - elaborate on unspoken thoughts (e. g. writing a diary entry, letter or interior monologue).

While writing

- Try to adapt to the style of the given text, e. g.
  - the language (spoken English, everyday English, informal English),
  - the characters and the way they talk and interact (Who says how much?, Is a character aggressive/sad/happy ...?, How do the characters talk to each other?, etc.),
  - the narrator's comments, descriptions and explanations.
- For a play, add stage directions and props (*Requisiten*) to illustrate where the action takes place, what the characters wear and look like and how they behave and interact.
- Employ dialogue and make the characters interact; they can use feedback questions and phrases, interrupt each other, yell at each other, etc.

Colours used for markings and labellings in the texts:

- content → **blue**
- stylistic devices → **red**
- narrative/structural devices → **orange**
- allusions/symbols/references → **green**

Practise ... Writing a Continuation of a Fictional Text

Sam Graham-Felsen

Green

David Greenfeld, the protagonist of the novel, is one of the few white students at Martin Luther King Jr. Middle School in Boston, Massachusetts, because his hippie parents don't want David to grow up as a privileged and spoiled child. In the excerpt from the novel, David describes his first day at his new school.

narrator: ____________ ____________

David and Kev: ____________ ____________

mode of presentation: ____________ ____________

____________ ____________ ____________

I am the white boy at the Martin Luther King Middle. Well, one of two. Kev, my best friend and the biggest dick[1] I know, is the other. But if you had to pick just one, it'd be me.

There is a public middle school in Boston that white kids actually go to – the Timilty – but me and Kev lost the lotto to get in there. I begged my parents to put me in a private school instead of the King, but they wouldn't budge[2]. They "believe in public schools," even when they're a mad ghetto.

The first day of school starts in an hour. If I had a best outfit, I'd be rocking[3] it, but my closet's a disaster of second-hand pants, free tees, and sale-bin[4] sneakers. Kev has an arsenal of stonewashed jeans and silk button-downs. He cops[5] a fresh pair of kicks[6] every couple months and he's debuting[7] some Air Force 1s[8] today. I'll be carrying a toothbrush and a travel shampoo in my pocket so I can scrub spots off my year-old Filas[9]. [...]

The thing about my house is that it's on top of a hill. At one end of the hill, there's a park – probably the nicest in the city – called the Arboretum. It's huge, manicured, owned and operated by Harvard U[10]. Pops says it has one of the biggest collections of tree species in the world. You can see the Arbs from my attic – endless green, spilling into the horizon. But from the opposite side of my attic, you'll see stream rising out of the tops of dark towers. Those are the projects[11] at the other end of my block, the Robert Gould Shaw Homes. Even though it takes me twice as long from my crib[12] to Centre Street, where all the stores – and my bus stop – are, I've been looping past[13] the Arbs all summer to avoid the back of the Shaw Homes. I'd take the direct route, but practically every time I walk past the PJs[14] these days, someone stutter-stomps[15] toward me, shouts, *"Fuck you lookin' at, white boy?"* and I end up jetting all the way back home. My first day at the King's gonna be bad enough. I'm not trying to get jacked[16] before I even make it to school. [...]

[1] **dick** (*offensive*) a stupid person – [2] **to budge** to change your opinion – [3] **to rock sth.** (*sl.*) to wear sth. and look good in it – [4] **sale-bin** container full of a special offer; buy it now – [5] **to cop** (*infml.*) to buy sth. – [6] **kicks** (*infml.*) shoes – [7] **to debut** to show in public for the first time – [8] **Air Force 1** expensive Nike sneakers – [9] **Fila** Italian label; sneakers – [10] **Harvard U** Harvard University; prestigious university at the US East Coast – [11] **projects** *Sozialwohnungen* – [12] **crib** (*sl., US*) home – [13] **to loop past** to make a curve around sb./sth. – [14] **PJs** (*abbr.*) short form of "projects" – [15] **to stutter-stomp** *entgegentrampeln, attackieren* – [16] **to get jacked** (*infml.*) to be robbed

choice of words:

We walk through the front doors and I take a whiff[17] of familiar funk[18]. The King smells just like elementary did: a sour blend of mop juice and soft beans in murky water. A cane[19]-carrying black dude[20] in a brown corduroy blazer shakes everyone's hands as we file past him. He greets the seventh and eighth graders formally, by last name, and he even pronounces the Spanish ones with decent rolling r's. To the sixth graders, he says, "Welcome to the King. I'm your principal, Dr. Jackson. And you are?"

the principal:

"Dave," I say.

"Oh yes. David … give me a second … Mr. *Greenfeld*?" he says, enunciating[21] the shit out of my last name. "Had a nice chat with your parents last year at the open house. You ever need anything – *anything* – you come see me now, okay?"

reference:

I nod, eyeing the student-painted mural[22] on the wall behind him. It's supposed to be Martin Luther King standing in front of the Lincoln Memorial, but the way they drew him – wide-open mouth, bugged-out eyes, stiff raised arms – makes it look like he's trying to step to someone instead of uniting the races. The quote bubble bursting from his mouth says, "What's *YOUR* dream?"

characteristics:

"Let's make sure you're all in the right place," homeroom teacher, Ms. Ansley, a small black lady with a helmet of dark, dyed[23] reddish hair, says. She calls attendance[24], hands us star-speckled nameplates, and assigns us to our seats. To my right is Carmen Garcia. She has pink glasses and shiny black hair, and she's wearing a flowery dress with ruffled[25] shoulders. The outfit makes her look like a substitute teacher, but beneath all that she's kind of cute. To my left is Kaleem Gunderson, a tall, light-skinned kid with faint freckles and a high-top fade[26]. He's got the phattest[27] gear of anyone in the class: a Chicago Bulls tracksuit, matching red Jordans[28], and a thick gold chain with a roaring-lion piece. For once I'm happy about my last name; I'm gonna be sitting next to this don[29] all year.

Carmen Garcia:

Kaleem Gunderson:

"Why I gotta be next to the white boy?" he grumbles to himself.

The white boy – see? Kev's in our class, too, but he's half-Armenian. He has spiky[30] black hair and lip scruff[31] and sometimes people mistake him for Puerto Rican. I have curly blond hair, pink cheeks, and pale blue eyes. No one mistakes me for shit.

Ms. Ansley walks to the chalkboard and slowly writes the word *why*. "My favorite word in the world. A three-letter word – a three-letter question! Why. Why? *Why!*"

Why?:

questions:

The class stares, confused. I assume this is some kind of motivational speech. When you come up in the middle schools, all you ever get is motivationally spoken to. Our classroom is covered with the same inspiring posters we had in elementary, too. One of them shows a hyped-up white kid ski-jumping off a mountain of books. Another says, AMBITION: IT'S CONTAGIOUS[32]!

"Why are we here?" she finally says. "Let's see some hands. No right or wrong answers to this one."

"We got no choice," says Kaleem.

Ms. Ansley smiles and says, "True enough."

"So we get our diplomas," a girl behind me says.

"All right," says Ms. Ansley. "Anyone else?"

[17] **whiff of sth.** a slight smell of sth. – [18] **funk** a strong bad smell – [19] **cane** *Stock* – [20] **dude** (*sl., US*) man – [21] **to enunciate** (*fml.*) to pronounce words very clearly – [22] **mural** a large picture that has been painted on a wall – [23] **dyed** *gefärbt* – [24] **to call attendance** to make a record of who is present – [25] **ruffled** *gerüscht* – [26] **high-top fade** a haircut with a long, flat afro on top and very short sides – [27] **phat** (*sl.*) very good – [28] **Jordans** expensive Nike sneakers – [29] **don** (*infml.*) head of a mafia family – [30] **spiky** *stachelig* – [31] **lip scruff** a very short moustache – [32] **contagious** *ansteckend*

The kid from our bus stop, the one with the C's mag[33], raises his hand. I glance at his nameplate. MARLON WELLINGS.

"To learn?"

Kaleem snorts[34] into his fist.

"Okay, Marlon, and *why* learn?"

"To get smarter."

"Why?" she says.

"So we can, like, choose better?"

"Why's that important?" she asks, her grin getting bigger.

Marlon pauses. His big eyes roll upward in thought.

"So we don't get tricked as easy?"

"See, now we're onto something. That's a good answer, especially with the election coming up. Took some *whying*, but we got somewhere. *Whying*. That means playing your own devil's advocates[35]. Not just thinking, *On the other hand*, but *On the other hand*, too. The good stuff, the worthwhile thinking, usually doesn't come till at least the third round, the third why. My number one goal is to get you to start *whying* on your own. My number two goal is to get you out of here."

motivation:

She starts passing out fat test prep books.

"You're my advanced class, and as far as I'm concerned each and every one of you should be aiming for Latin. Don't think I don't love you all, but I prefer not to see your pretty faces in these halls come seventh grade. Unless, of course, you want to come back and *visit* and tell everyone how you're doing at Latin."

Boston Latin is the best public high school in the city – by far. You have to take a three-hour test to get in. I suck[36] at those bubble sheets[37]. I look over at Kev, who's resting his bows on his test prep book. I know he won't ever bother[38] to crack[39] it. Kev is a standardized test genius. Marlon's already got his book open, running a finger along the text.

Boston Latin:

"I know you all hate these kinds of tests, but I'm telling you, the more you practice, the more you're gonna learn the tricks – or, rather, how *not* to get tricked. Kids from all over the city – private-school kids, too – are going to be scrambling[40] for spots[41], and you don't wanna lose out because you were too lazy to take the practice tests. I want you start studying *tonight*, okay? Because if you get into Latin, you're going to college guaranteed. And let me tell you something else. You might even get into Harvard[42]."

allusion:

Marlon grins and I notice he has a gap in his front teeth like I do.

from *Green* by Sam Graham-Felsen. Random House, New York 2018, pp. 3 ff.

COMPREHENSION

Read the excerpt from the novel closely and take notes on:

- David Greenfeld and his family,
- David's way to school,
- Martin Luther King Jr. Middle School,
- David's classmates,
- Ms. Ansley, David's teacher and her way of teaching and motivating the students.

Take notes in the margin of the text and highlight or underline relevant information and key words and phrases in the text.

[33] **C's mag** a type of magazine featuring machine guns and assault rifles – [34] **to snort** *schnaufen, prusten* – [35] **devil's advocate** sb. who supports the less accepted opinion to make people discuss and consider it in more detail – [36] **to suck** (*obscene*) to be very bad at sth. – [37] **bubble sheet** (*infml.*) a multiple choice test – [38] **to bother** to try to do sth. – [39] **to crack** (*infml.*) to open a new book – [40] **to scramble for sth.** to move quickly in panic – [41] **spot** place; here: a place to study at a good university – [42] **Harvard** prestigious university at the US East Coast

ACTIVITIES

In the school cafeteria, during lunch break, David and his friend Kev are sitting at the same table with some of their classmates who all have different ethnicities.
Because of their skin colour and different social background, David and Kev stand out from the other students and have become like characters from a curio show (*Kuriositätenkabinett*).
Imagine

- **what the students might be talking about,**
- **what they want to know about each other and are curious about,**
- **what they are thinking about each other and the situation,**
- **which possible conflicts might arise out of this situation.**

Tip: Be careful about the use of language. Naturally, the students speak everyday English and sometimes even informal English with each other. However, be careful with using slang or grammatically incorrect English. At least the passages (spoken) by the narrator should be written in Standard English.

Step 1:
Collect information given in the excerpt about David, Kev and their classmates.

David	Kev
• *curly, blond hair*	• *half-Armenian*
• hippie parents	• new trendy style
• only old, second hand clothes	• David's best friend
•	•
•	•

Carmen Garcia	Kaleem Gunderson
• *Hispanic*	• tall
• shiny black hair	• light skinned
• pink glasses	• faint freckles
• flowery dress	• high top fade
• →	• expensive outfit

Marlon Wellings
• *black*
• *lives in the projects*
• vilont
• nasty
•

Step 2:
Have in mind that this is first day at school for David and the other students. Think about what they

- are curious about,
- tell each other about themselves or try to hide from the others,
- ask each other or want to know about the others.

Step 3:

The creative writing task requires you to imagine what the characters of the text at hand would do or say. Here are some ideas to help you put yourself in their position:

- Some of the students might be ashamed of their social background (e.g. the projects, living in a nice neighbourhood like David) and might not want to talk about it.
- Some students might be proud of what they have achieved in school so far …
- It might be difficult for David and Kev to be the only white students …
- David seems to be embarrassed by his second-hand clothes, his hippie parents, etc.
- Some students might be very ambitious (Latin, Harvard) and talk about their future plans or dreams.
- Students might talk about Martin Luther King Jr. and their (parents') role model …

Step 4:

Now, write a continuation of the excerpt from the novel and let the students talk and interact.

Tip: Be careful to follow the structural pattern of the excerpt from the novel.

- Vary the mode of presentation (see Info box).
- Give your dialogue and text a clear structure.
- Think about a climax or unexpected twists and turns in the course of the action.

Info – Mode of presentation

a) panoramic: the narrator tells the story as a condensed series of events, summarizing in a few sentences what happens over a longer period of time

b) scenic: the author shows an event in detail as it occurs, using dialogue, depicting thoughts and emotions, describing the scene, etc.

Your dialogue or text may have a surprising, funny, tragicomic or sad and melancholic ending.

Your continuation:

The bell rings. "Okay let's have a short break." Ms Ansley announses.

Prepare for … Writing a Newspaper Commentary/Blog Post

A written comment or blog post expresses your personal opinion on a certain topic or issue. It should have a **clear structure** and be based on arguments.

Snake blogging.

Before writing

- Collect information about the issue or topic you are going to comment on.
- Collect arguments in favour of and against a certain topic or issue (cf. Hourglass principle, p. 74).
- Structure your thoughts **systematically**.
- Give your comment a clear structure:

introduction (introductory remarks, raising a question, stating a view)
↓
main part (juxtaposing arguments backed up by examples and facts)
↓
conclusion (summing up, giving a final result)

While writing

- Use the simple present as the predominant tense.
- Employ rhetorical devices to emphasize your view (e.g. repetition, rhetorical questions, climax, alliteration, etc.).
- Begin and conclude your text with a concise (*prägnant*) remark or statement that stays in the reader's mind.

Colours used for markings and labellings in the texts:

- content → blue
- stylistic devices → red
- narrative/structural devices → orange
- allusions/symbols/references → green

Practise ... Commenting on a Topic and Writing a Review

Richard Brody

"Honeyland," Reviewed: A Gripping, Frustrating Documentary About a Beekeeper's Fragile Isolation

Honeyland is a 2019 Macedonian documentary film which portrays the life of Hatidže Muratova and her lonely life as a beekeeper in a remote mountain village. By documenting Hatidže's life and the depletion of her bees through ignorant and greedy neighbours, the filmmakers thematize current topics such as the exploitation of natural resources and loss of biodiversity. The documentary was nominated for two Oscars in 2020 and received numerous international awards.

The documentary "Honeyland," about a beekeeper in rural Macedonia whose livelihood is threatened by the actions of new neighbors, has many of the virtues of a good dramatic feature. Its narrative construction depicts extraordinary tensions and conflicts with a clarity and coherence[1] that a screenwriter might dream of. At the same time, the film's dramatic power comes at the expense of the reportorial[2] side of documentary filmmaking. It's as if the filmmakers, Tamara Kotevska and Ljubomir Stefanov, recognized the allure[3] of their subject as the action unfolded, and then, whether in the filming or in the editing of their footage[4] (four hundred-plus hours' worth, cut down to an eighty-seven-minute feature), molded it to familiar forms of movie drama. The result is a film that's in equal measure gripping and frustrating, a work of nonfiction in which the elision[5] of many factual elements, in the interest of compact dramaturgy[6], makes an extraordinary true story feel fabricated.

introduction: ____________ ____________

criticism: ____________ ____________

A woman carrying a bundle on her back is seen, from far above, walking alone on a desolate plain along a path cut unevenly through dry grass; and then from below; and then, again, from a different high angle. She reaches a steep rock face by climbing on a narrow ledge[7] onto which the camera operator follows her, too. As I watched the woman approaching the rocks, pulling a honeycomb from a dark compartment behind a stone plaque[8], and scooping[9] bees by the cupful into a basket, I found myself wondering what she thought of the filmmakers who were following her on this perilous[10] mission – how she and they arranged the shooting, and, from a Heisenbergian[11] perspective, what effect the filmmakers' presence had on her activities and her ideas.

reference: ____________ ____________

perspective: ____________ ____________

The woman's name is Hatidze. (Her last name, Muratova, is seen in the end credits.) She was born, she says, in 1964; she has, apparently, spent her entire life in this craggy[12] farm region of the former Yugoslav republic. She lives with her mother, who's bedridden[13] and ill, in a stone house with no electricity or running water. Her mother, Nazife – whose name is never heard in the course of the film – has an oozing[14] and apparently sightless eye and a grave[15] bleeding wound near it, on the side of her face, which is bound with a compress and a towel. The family is of Turkish ethnicity, and speaks Turkish.

Hatidže: ____________ ____________

[1] **coherence** *Zusammenhang, Stimmigkeit* – [2] **reportorial** like a reporter – [3] **allure** the quality of being attractive and interesting – [4] **footage** recorded video material – [5] **elision** *Auslassung* – [6] **dramaturgy** the art of writing and putting on plays for the theatre – [7] **ledge** *Absatz* – [8] **plaque** *Platte* – [9] **to scoop** *schaufeln* – [10] **perilous** (*fml.*) extremely dangerous – [11] **Heisenberg(ian)** of physicist Werner Heisenberg, here: the "observer effect" (when sth. is watched, its behaviour changes) – [12] **craggy** *zerklüftet, schroff* – [13] **bedridden** *bettlägerig* – [14] **to ooze** to leak slowly – [15] **grave** seriously bad

device:

____

____

Hatidze, who never married and has no children, ekes[16] out a living for herself and her mother by keeping bees and gathering and bottling their honey. Hatidze's methods are intimate and humane; she's endowed[17] with a loving touch that, seemingly, the bees recognize – she works with them barehanded and appears never to be stung. She speaks to them and sings to them, but, above all, she nurtures and nourishes them, telling them, "half for you, half for me" – she doesn't deplete[18] their supply of honey to maximize her short-term income but treats the hives that she sustains[19] on another rock wall, alongside her home, with familial care.

Hatidze and her mother live in apparent isolation, without friends, other family, or neighbors. Then a string of trucks and a trailer struggle along a road to another stone house, diagonally across from hers – the Sam family, also of Turkish ethnicity, including a mother (Ljutvie), a father (Hussein), and seven children, ranging from toddlers to preteens. The family raises cattle and brings with it a large herd, and the family quickly befriends Hatidze. She plays with and teaches the children, talks with Ljutvie and Hussein, and, when he visits her, shows him her hive. Hussein asks her about money – what she gets for her honey – and, with that apparently innocent question, it's obvious, after a very gradual and protracted[20] setup, that the drama is about to begin. Approximately ten euros per jar, she responds, and, if "Honeyland" were a cartoon, Hussein would suddenly get euro symbols in his eyes.

Moments later, he's seen unloading from a truck a set of boxes and frames used in commercial beekeeping. Hatidze, friendly and helpful but also wary[21], cautions him to leave half of his honey for his bees – because otherwise they'll attack her bees for their honey. It's no spoiler to relate that this is exactly what happens, though the way that it happens – in its effect on Hatidze and her mother, in the commercial details that drive Hussein to mercenary[22] despair, and in its effect on relationships within the Sam family, too – unfolds with a novelistic intricacy[23] and tightly sprung[24] dramatic mechanism. Just in outlining the conflict here, I find myself caught up again in its destructive power, its brewing enmities[25], and its overarching[26], tragic sense of the disturbance of cosmic order.

advice:

____

____

choice of words:

____

____

Yet there is a price – or, perhaps, not a price but merely a needless sacrifice – that comes with tying this mighty narrative knot[27]. Kotevska and Stefanov give little sense of the surrounding world in which the film's participants live, and what the filmmakers do show tends to frustrate rather than satisfy the viewer's curiosities. Hatidze travels by train to the country's capital, Skopje, to sell honey, sitting on the trip, as if by calculated cinematic contrast, next to a teen punk with spiky green hair. Speaking with one of her retailers, who is Albanian, she says that all the other Albanians and Turks have left her village, that she and her mother are the only ones left. But we never find out what kind of crisis or what circumstances led to this exodus[28], or how isolated Hatidze's life actually is. […] Her life is depicted as one of complete autonomy, as if her rocky corner were long untouched by any civil authority. […]

criticism:

____

____

[16] **to eke out a living** (*phr. v.*) to barely get enough to survive – [17] **endowed** *ausgestattet* – [18] **to deplete** to empty sth. – [19] **to sustain** to keep alive – [20] **protracted** made to last longer than necessary – [21] **wary** not completely trusting – [22] **mercenary** *profitgierig* – [23] **intricacy** the quality of having many complicated small details – [24] **tightly sprung** full of tension – [25] **enmity** very strong hate – [26] **overarching** dominating and affecting all other areas – [27] **narrative knot** the way a plot is structured and unfolded – [28] **exodus** the departure of many people from a place

device:

irony:

choice of words:

criticism:

Hatidze's solitude is one of the film's prime subjects and also its dramatic mainspring, and its details and practicalities[29] are merely hinted at, and utterly unexplored, throughout. One of the Sam boys becomes Hatidze's companion in her apiary[30] adventures, and in one conversation she laments that she doesn't have a son like him. Not long thereafter, Hatidze asks her mother why she turned down offers of marriage that were brought for Hatidze, long ago, by a matchmaker. Nazife gives a poignant[31] response – that she didn't turn the offers down, but Hatidze's late father did – but the exchange has a contrived[32] feeling. Has she never before confronted her mother on this central life matter? We don't know, because the filmmakers wouldn't dare disturb the sealed-off[33] observational purity of their storytelling with even so much as an interview question. [...]

The filmmakers establish an agrarian fantasy of perfect rustic isolation, a place of Edenic purity[34] in which more than Hatidze's own loving enterprise, her livelihood, is threatened – what's spoiled is paradise itself. [...] This is no mere theoretical quibble[35] of documentary form; it's the relationship between experience and cinema, between what's happening and what's seen. It's a relationship that, despite their daring[36], perceptive[37], nuanced, and empathetic[38] work, the filmmakers didn't respect.

https://www.newyorker.com/culture/the-front-row/honeyland-reviewed-a-gripping-frustrating-documentary-about-a-beekeepers-fragile-isolation, 1 August 2019 [05.04.2021]

COMPREHENSION

Read the article from *The New Yorker* and underline or highlight

a) information given on Hatidže's way of life as a beekeeper,

b) the description of the destruction of Hatidže's "paradise" by the Sam family,

c) criticism the author utters concerning

- the lack of information about the background of Hatidže's life (political, social, familial),
- the combination of the genres "documentary" and "movie drama".

Tip: As the article is rather complex because of its sophisticated language, be prepared to read it at least two times and structure it by taking notes in the margin of the page, using different colours (cf. box on p. 70).

Tip: To help you get a better impression of the film and its atmosphere, you can watch the film trailer which is provided on the webcode belonging to your students' book (WES-121500-021).

ACTIVITIES

Write a comment (a blog entry) in response to the article in which you critically state whether (or not) you

a) share the author's criticism of the way the documentary was filmed and how the story of Hatidže is presented,

b) approve of films and documentaries like *Honeyland* which try to make the audience aware of current issues and problems.

Tip: As a comment falls into the category of argumentative texts, it requires a clear structure and the use of rhetorical devices.

[29] **practicality** *Durchführbarkeit* – [30] **apiary** ['eɪpiəri] *Bienenhaus* – [31] **poignant** causing a very sharp feeling of sadness – [32] **contrived** artificial and difficult to believe – [33] **to seal sth. off** (*phr. v.*) to prevent people from entering a dangerous building or area – [34] **Edenic purity** the quality of being perfect like in paradise (*Eden*) – [35] **quibble** minor complaint or criticism – [36] **daring** brave and taking risks – [37] **perceptive** very good at noticing and understanding things that other people do not notice – [38] **emphatic** *einfühlsam*

Step 1:
Against the background of the magazine article at hand and our impression of the film trailer, take notes on the author's criticism of the film in the grid below.

author's criticism	my view/comment
• *documentary was turned into a movie drama*	→
• *elision of factual elements*	→
• *story feels fabricated*	→
•	→
•	→
•	→
•	→
•	→
•	→

Step 2:
Reflect on the author's criticism and add your thoughts in right column of the grid.

Step 3:
Think about a concise introduction in which you raise a controversial question or make an introductory (provocative) remark or statement on the matter or the film.

Examples:
- *(To) Bee or No(t) (to) Bee, that is the question here.*
- *Documentary or drama – what shall it be?*

Step 4:
In the main part of your comment, state and juxtapose (*gegenüberstellen*) the pros and cons of the topic.

Tip: Do not just state your opinions. Instead, collect valid arguments and examples that support your view.

Step 5:
Decide on the structure of your argumentation:
- listing structure,
- antithetical structure,
- progressive structure,

and sort your material accordingly.

Tip: The so-called "Hourglass principle" can help to form an antithetical line of argument.

Hourglass principle

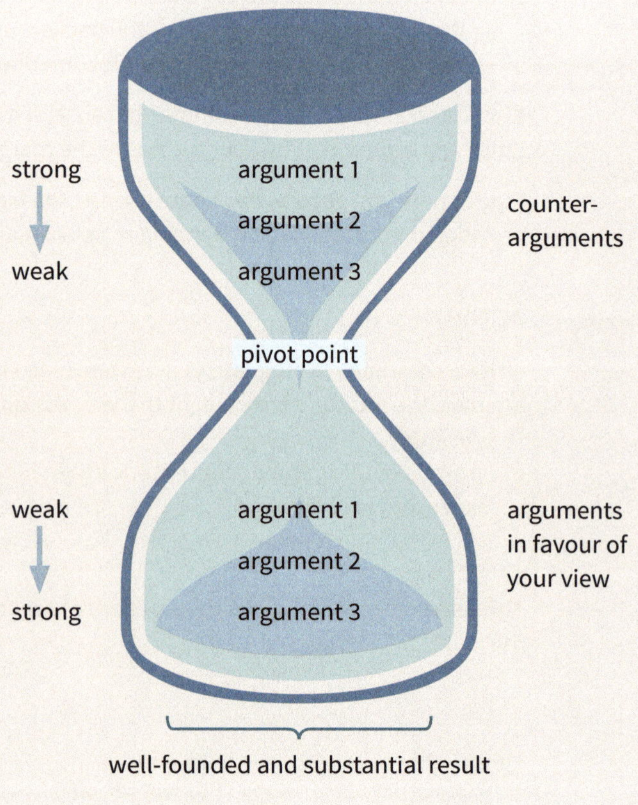

Step 6:
Collect ideas about rhetorical devices that support your line of argument.

Examples:
- *rhetorical question: Can mankind afford the ongoing mass extinction of species?*
- *climax/alliteration: dramatic, disgusting, disastrous*

Step 7:
Finally, write a coherent text of about 250 words in which you comment on the author's criticism and state your opinion on films like *Honeyland*.

Tips on vocab

on the one hand … on the other hand ■ on the contrary ■ compared to/with ■ to be in contrast with ■ to make/draw a comparison between … and ■ to relate … to/with ■ to distinguish between ■ to tell the difference between ■ to draw a distinction between

Your text:

Prepare for ... Writing a Newspaper Article

In general, a newspaper article aims at informing the readership, thus providing answers to questions (who – what – where – when – why).
Newspaper articles should be easy to read, objective and present unbiased facts and information.

Basic elements of newspaper articles:
- **headline** (catching the reader's attention)
- **sub-headline** (structuring the article)
- **columns/paragraphs** (all paragraphs relate to the main idea)
- **pictures/photos/graphics/visuals** (illustration, proof)
- **following paragraphs** (provide answers to the questions, develop the main idea)
- **information** (clear, concise, factual)
- **language** (precise, clear sentence structure)
- **grammatical tense** (usually past tense, direct speech, reported speech)
- **references** (to what people said, to sources)

Before writing

- Do research on the matter and its background.
- List your potential sources and sort them.

While writing

- Write your **lead-in** (the introductory paragraph → answering the w-questions).
- Think of an interesting **headline** that catches the readers' attention and evokes their interest.
- Write the **body** (= main part) of the article.
  - Structure it into paragraphs of 4 – 5 lines.
  - Use the technique "1 paragraph – 1 idea".
- Give your article a **clear line of thought**, e.g. g. write about the events and/or people in a chronological order or a topical order (e. g. the camp, children, refugee policy, etc.).

Colours used for markings and labellings in the texts:
- content → blue
- stylistic devices → red
- narrative/structural devices → orange
- allusions/symbols/references → green

Practise ... Writing a Newspaper Article – The Story Behind the Picture

Diego Herrera

Refugee Children at Camp Moria, Lesbos, Greece

Camp Moria was the largest refugee camp in Europe until it burned down in September 2020. The organization Doctors Without Borders called it "the worst refugee camp on earth" because until 2020, at least 13,000 people lived there, among them 6,000 to 7,000 children, despite the fact that the camp was built for just 3,000 people. After detecting COVID-19 cases in the camp in 2020, the situation escalated and refugees demonstrated and demanded to be evacuated. The Vice Chairman of the UN Human Rights Council, Jean Ziegler, said that people had to live in the camp like animals and that Camp Moria was "the recreation of concentration camps on European soil". UNICEF declared the living conditions of children in Moria a fundamental violation of children's rights.

background: ______________________

facial expression: ______________________

Children playing in Camp Moria, an island 10 kilometres from Greece, where about 10,000 people live.
Photo: Diego Herrera, 2020

source: ______________________

eye-catcher: ______________________

Tips on vocab

children enjoying themselves ■ playing with old/self-made makeshift toys ■ a plastic toy motor buggy ■ a push cart ■ tents made of plastic sheeting ■ dried out trees and shrubbery/bushes ■ dirt road ■ rubbish ■ plastic bottles ■ drainage pipes

COMPREHENSION

Before writing the article, take some time to concentrate on the photograph and do some research on the (political, social) background of the photograph.
Describe the photograph in detail, paying attention to:

- the overall atmosphere it conveys,
- the people and their actions, body language and facial expressions,
- striking eye-catchers and visual symbols,
- the surroundings.

Tip: Use the Tips on vocab box and the information below the photograph.

Do further research on Camp Moria and take notes on:

- the causes and reasons for building the camp,
- the scandalous, disastrous living conditions of the migrants and refugees in Moria,
- the children living in Camp Moria,
- the evacuation of children after the fire of 2020.

ACTIVITIES

You are a journalist for an international youth magazine and are asked to write a story about the photograph taken in Camp Moria in 2020.
Write an article for the magazine that captures the situation and includes additional information on the children and refugees of Camp Moria as well as the political background.

Step 1:
Decide on the style of your article and whether it should be more informative or more emotional.

Step 2:
Inform your readers about the striking contrast between the emotions the playing children convey and the reality of life in the camp.
Use a dictionary and look up words that describe the difference.

children	reality/life in the camp
• *enjoying themselves*	• *being trapped*
• *playing, having fun*	• *trash everywhere*
•	•
•	•
•	•
•	•
•	•
•	•
•	•
•	•

Step 3:
Describe the situation of the children and the people living in the camp as precisely as possible. Use a dictionary and find the respective formal and informal synonyms of adjectives, nouns and phrases you want to use in the article.
Usually, the more formal words have more syllables and derive (*abstammen von*) from Latin or French. In contrast, many of the everyday language words are quite short (monosyllabic).

Examples:

adjectives/nouns/phrases	everyday/informal English	formal English
fröhlich		*joyful*
hilflos	*helpless*	
helfen		*to support*
Hilfe		

Step 4:
If you have access to a computer, you may design and type-set the magazine article on screen. Think about a layout that matches your chosen type of magazine and arrange necessary elements (e. g. columns, photos, an interview, banner headline, etc.) accordingly.

Step 5:
Finally, write the textual elements of your magazine article, proofread it and make sure to cross-check the factual information, figures, etc. in order to have valid and correct information.
Do not forget to cite the sources you have used.

Prepare for ... Writing a Letter to the Editor

A **letter to the editor** is a **formal letter** that has various functions:

- Responding to an article you have read and stating your opinion on the matter.
- Expressing your criticism or support of the view taken by the author or publication.
- Commenting on a current issue.
- Correcting a perceived error or misinterpretation.

"THEY PUBLISHED MY LETTER ABOUT RECYCLING NEWSPAPERS."

Before writing

- Read the article or publication thoroughly, highlight or underline the most relevant parts and take notes on them.
- Do further research on the matter to back up your letter.
- **Keep in mind** to include the following elements in your letter:
  - your name, address, telephone number and e-mail address (in the letterhead)
  - the name of the article you are responding to (in the subject line)
  - a salutation (e.g. Dear Sir or Madam); do not write a comma
  - a capital letter at the beginning of the body of the letter
  - paragraphs, separated by a free line
  - a complimentary close (e.g. Yours sincerely/(Best) Regards); do not write a comma
  - your signature below

While writing

- Do not write a lengthy argument; instead, get to the point and be formal.
- Use Standard English.
- Limit your letter to two or three paragraphs: introduction – body (arguments, examples – conclusion).
- Do not be overly emotional; instead, write in a matter-of-fact style (i.e. avoiding emotive language, adjectives, etc.).
- If you don't want your name to be published, state so clearly.

Colours used for markings and labellings in the texts:

- content → **blue**
- stylistic devices → **red**
- narrative/structural devices → **orange**
- allusions/symbols/references → **green**

Practise ... Responding to an Online Article

Christopher Sherman et al.

US Held Record Number of Migrant Children in Custody[1] in 2019

In 2018, the US Department of Justice implemented a "zero tolerance" policy toward illegal border crossing which aimed at intensifying the criminal prosecution of people caught entering the US illegally. So-called "unauthorized" immigrant parents were separated from their children at the border, both groups being held in US custody. While the parents had to serve time in criminal custody, the children were often detained in "border control holding cells" or given to foster parents without informing the parents about their children's whereabouts.
After massive protests and complaints from the US population, politicians and civil rights organisations the policy was officially reversed at the end of 2018.

COMAYAGUA, Honduras – The 3-year-old girl traveled for weeks cradled[2] in her father's arms, as he set out to seek asylum in the United States. Now she won't even look at him.

After being forcibly separated at the border by government officials, sexually abused in U.S. foster care[3] and deported, the once bright and beaming girl arrived back in Honduras withdrawn, anxious and angry, convinced her father abandoned her.

He fears their bond is forever broken.

"I think about this trauma staying with her too, because the trauma has remained with me and still hasn't faded," he said, days after their reunion.

This month, new government data shows the little girl is one of an unprecedented 69,550 migrant children held in U.S. government custody over the past year, enough infants, toddlers[4], kids and teens to overflow the typical NFL stadium. That's more children detained[5] away from their parents than any other country, according to United Nations researchers. And it's happening even though the U.S. government has acknowledged[6] that being held in detention can be traumatic for children, putting them at risk of long-term physical and emotional damage.

Some of these migrant children who were in government custody this year have already been deported. Some have reunited with family in the U.S., where they're trying to go to school and piece their lives back together. About 4,000 are still in government custody, some in large, impersonal shelters[7]. And more arrive every week.

The nearly 70,000 migrant children who were held in government custody this year – up 42 percent in fiscal[8] year 2019 from 2018 – spent more time in shelters and away from their families than in prior years. The Trump administration's series of strict immigration policies has increased the time children spend in detention, despite the government's own acknowledgment that it does them harm. In 2013, Australia detained 2,000 children during a surge of maritime arrivals. In Canada, immigrant children are separated from their parents only as a last resort; 155 were detained in 2018. In the United Kingdom, 42 migrant children were put in shelters in 2017, according to officials in those countries. [...]

device: ____________________ ____________________

example/ human interest: ____________________ ____________________

device: ____________________ ____________________

international numbers: ____________________ ____________________

[1] **custody** *Gewahrsam* – [2] **to cradle** to hold closely – [3] **foster care** *Pflegeunterbringung* – [4] **toddler** young child, esp. one that recently learned to walk – [5] **to detain** to force sb. to stay in an official place, such as a police station or prison – [6] **to acknowledge** to accept that sth. is true – [7] **shelter** *Unterkunft* – [8] **fiscal** connected with public money

One Honduran teen who was held in a large detention center[9] for four months before reuniting with his mother said that, as each day passed, his fear and anxiety grew.

"There was something there that made us feel desperate. It was freedom. We wanted to be free," he recalled. "There was despair everywhere."

Another Honduran teen, who arrived in the U.S. at 16 and was detained in a series of increasingly secure shelters for more than a year, said he saw his peers harm themselves.

quotes:

"They would cry sometimes, alone, or they would hit themselves against the wall," he said. "I thought that was because of them being here for such a long time."

The teens spoke on condition of anonymity out of concerns for their safety.

The 3-year-old Honduran girl was taken from her father when immigration officials caught them near the border in Texas in March 2019 and sent her to government-funded foster care. The father had no idea where his daughter was for three panicked weeks. It was another month before a caregiver put her on the phone but the girl, who turned 4 in government custody, refused to speak, screaming in anger. [...]

choice of words:

The U.S. government calls migrant children held without their parents "Unaccompanied Alien[10] Children" – UAC in bureaucratic jargon. Federal law requires the Department of Health and Human Services' Office of Refugee Resettlement to provide them food and shelter, and medical and mental health care. But the HHS Office of Inspector General found there aren't enough clinicians or specialized care in shelters holding migrant children.

HHS spokesman Mark Weber said that, with the largest number of migrant children in their program's history, "you must give credit to the Office of Refugee Resettlement and the shelter network staff for managing a program that was able to rapidly expand and unify[11] the largest number of kids ever, all in an incredibly difficult environment."

In an urgent request[12] to fund an emergency shelter earlier this year, HHS warned "Without a way to provide these services, there is an unacceptable risk that thousands of UAC would be without their basic human needs, which would result in injury/death of children." [...]

U.S. immigration authorities have separated more than 5,400 children from their parents at the Mexico border, before, during and after a controversial "zero tolerance" policy was enacted and then ended in the spring of 2018. [...]

https://apnews.com/article/us-news-ap-top-news-honduras-trauma-immigration-015702afdb4d4fbf85cf5070cd2c6824, 12 November 2019 [20.07.2021]

COMPREHENSION

Read the magazine article and take notes on:

- the examples of Honduran migrant children and teenagers
- the information on international immigration policies
- the problems that the HHS department has in organizing their work

Tip: Take notes in the margin and underline or highlight relevant information given in the article using different colours (see box on p. 80).

[9] **detention center** here: a place where people who have entered a country without the necessary documents can be kept for short periods of time; *Auffanglager* – [10] **alien** coming from a different country – [11] **to unify** to bring together; to combine – [12] **request** the act of asking for sth.

ACTIVITIES

Being a teenager yourself, write a letter to the editor on the controversial topic, expressing your personal view on
- **the US government's zero tolerance policy of 2018/2019,**
- **the treatment of migrant children globally.**

Tip: Although you should generally aim at expressing your thoughts straightforwardly and frankly, try to use a more neutral language register and avoid being too informal so as not to appear judgemental or biased. Use a dictionary to find appropriate words and double-check certain formulations if you are not sure about them.

Step 1:
Study the tips given on page 80 on how to write a formal letter.

Step 2:
Do further research on how migrant children are treated internationally to back up your letter.

Step 3:
Begin your letter by referring to the magazine article and pointing out your motivation to write the letter.

Example:
Being a teenager/young adult myself, I read your article published in … on … with great interest … The examples given of the traumatic experiences of … were really shocking. I would like to … Some years ago, Germany accepted … migrants and at our school …

Tips on vocab

- I was really surprised and shocked to find out that …
- I read a very informative article about …
- What would it be like if …?
- How can we ignore or even tolerate …?
- From my own perspective …

Tip: In order to improve your fluency and make your English sound more natural you can employ certain phrases or expressions called "fillers". However, be careful not to overdo things and use too many fillers. You do not want to produce empty phrases.

Step 4:
Structure the body of your letter clearly and avoid unnecessary repetition. Include examples, arguments and references to support your view.

Tips on vocab

last but not least ■ in answer to that point ■ in general … in particular ■ to put it more clearly ■ it seems to me obvious that … ■ it appears to be evident … ■ what I'd like to say/emphasize is …

Step 5:
Conclude your letter with a summarizing sentence and an outlook on the issue, e.g. by asking a (rhetorical) question or making a suggestion to possible alternatives.

Example:
I would like to conclude my letter by expressing my understanding of the difficulty of handling this enormous task … However, in my view, the international community does have a strong obligation to help refugees in general – and children in particular – who are suffering from poverty, war, criminality … in their home countries …

Prepare for ... Mediating a Non-Fictional Text

Mediating a text from one language into another is different from simply translating it word for word. Instead, you are asked to
- **select the most relevant information,**
- give an analogous rendition (*sinngemäße Wiedergabe*) of a text,
- give additional information if needed (e.g. on culture, geography, politics, etc.),
- consider the **addressee's background**,
- consider the **type of text** you are required to write or speak (e.g. an e-mail, presentation, report, etc.).

While mediating

- Read or listen to the text **carefully** and watch out for or listen to **key words**.
- Underline or highlight relevant information which serves to answer your assignment.
- Leave out minor details.
- Put the relevant information into English, using **your own words** – but do not change the facts.
- **Use synonyms or paraphrases** if you do not know the exact (English) equivalent.
- Express difficult passages or phrases more simply, using everyday language if possible.

Colours used for markings and labellings in the texts:

- content → blue
- stylistic devices → red
- narrative/structural devices → orange
- allusions/symbols/references → green

Practise …
Mediating an Online Article About an Ongoing Trend

Eva Corino

Abi und was nun? – Die Generation Gap

Gap years have become very popular and affordable for young people and enable them to explore the world and make new experiences.

introduction: ____________ ____________

Immer mehr junge Frauen und Männer planen nach dem Abitur ein so genanntes „Gap Year“. Was treibt sie dazu und was fangen sie an mit dieser kostbaren Zwischenzeit?

Ausbrechen wollen sie, ausbrechen aus ihrer wattierten[1] Welt, ihre anhänglichen Eltern einmal abschütteln und sich ganz allein durchschlagen[2]. Ja, auch sie träumen von einem anderen Leben; aber anders als die Hippies in den siebziger Jahren sind die Abiturienten, die man vielleicht die „Gappies“ nennen könnte, nur Aussteiger[3] auf Zeit.

contrast: ____________ ____________

Emil: ____________ ____________

Emil zum Beispiel. Er hat als Deutscher mit seinen Eltern ein paar Jahre in Brasilien gewohnt. In einem Viertel von Rio de Janeiro, wo es Springbrunnen gab, die in gepflegten[4] Gärten vor sich hinplätscherten[5]. Dass Brasilien ein Land der eskalierenden Gewalt ist, das wusste er nur aus der Zeitung. Doch nach dem Abi wollte er das andere Brasilien kennenlernen. Deshalb bewarb er sich bei der Freiwilligenorganisation[6] „weltwärts“ und zog für ein Jahr in eine der ärmsten Favelas von Sao Paolo. Dort hat er sich um Straßenkinder gekümmert. Er hat mit ihnen Fußball gespielt, Hausaufgaben gemacht und von Deutschland erzählt. „Ich hab’ viel mehr von den Kindern gelernt als die Kinder von mir“, sagt Emil. „Ich habe gesehen, wie wenig man braucht, um zu leben, aber auch, wie wichtig es ist zu teilen.“

Ich hab’ viel mehr von den Kindern gelernt als die Kinder von mir. Ich habe gesehen, wie wenig man braucht, um zu leben, aber auch, wie wichtig es ist zu teilen. […]

Der Wunsch nach Entschleunigung[7]

Den Wunsch nach Entschleunigung der eigenen Bildungsbiographie teilt Emil mit vielen jungen Leuten. „Gap Year“ heißt das Zauberwort[8] dieser Generation, denn es beschwört[9] und bändigt[10] all ihre Nöte, Ambitionen und Sehnsüchte. Bei einer repräsentativen Umfrage[11] des Trendence-Instituts unter 21 000 Schülern, wollten nur 44 Prozent direkt nach dem Abitur ein Studium aufnehmen. 56 Prozent planten zunächst ein Jahr Pause, die große Mehrheit von ihnen im Ausland. […]

Der flammende[12] Idealismus der Bewegung „fridays-for-future“

Früher haben die Eltern oft die Ausbildung ihrer Kinder bestimmt. Heute verfolgen sie lieber einen individualistischen Ansatz[13], und

[1] padded (= safe and comfortable) – [2] to battle one’s way – [3] escapist, downshifter – [4] manicured – [5] to splash softly – [6] volunteer organisation – [7] deceleration – [8] magic word – [9] to bring to mind – [10] to tame – [11] poll – [12] blazing – [13] individualistic approach

choice of words:

als Sohn oder Tochter ist man sozusagen dazu verurteilt[14], frei zu sein. Hinzu kommt die Vielfalt der Möglichkeiten, die oft eine lähmende[15] Wirkung auf unsere Kinder hat. Allein in Deutschland werden 10000 grundständige Studiengänge[16] angeboten. Aber welcher ist der richtige? Die Explosion der Optionen steigert ihre Angst, sich falsch zu entscheiden, steigert die Gier, alles auf einmal zu wollen, und erschwert, sich mit einer einzigen Studienrichtung zufrieden zu geben. Mit dem Wohlstand wachsen die Ansprüche[17]: Das Studium muss hinführen zu einem Job, in dem man gut verdient, sich selbst verwirklicht – und außerdem ganz nebenbei noch die Welt rettet. Hier zeigt sich der flammende Idealismus der Bewegung „fridays-for-future", aber auch eine mächtige Prägung[18] durch die Konsumgesellschaft. […]

Die Grand Tour als Chance

Die Idee eines Lückenjahrs ist nicht neu. Schon seit der Renaissance existiert die Tradition der „Grand Tour", einer Bildungsreise[19] für die Söhne des europäischen Adels und gehobenen Bürgertums[20] durch Südeuropa oder ins Heilige Land. Sie sollte der Erziehung der Zöglinge[21] den letzten Schliff[22] geben, Wissen und Sprachkenntnis vertiefen, für neue Eindrücke und – unausgesprochen – wohl auch für das Erlangen einer gewissen erotischen Erfahrung sorgen.

past:

Nur wenige konnten sich so etwas leisten[23]. Heute ist die Grand Tour für immer größere Teile der deutschen Mittelschicht in Reichweite. Eine erstaunliche Entwicklung, die unseren Wohlstand sichtbar macht und das bereits erreichte Ausmaß der Globalisierung. Neu ist, dass inzwischen auch junge Frauen die Chance haben, so ihren Horizont zu erweitern – sich selbst in der Welt und die Welt in sich zu finden. Sie gehen als Au pair nach Kanada, machen work & travel in Australien, unternehmen eine Rucksackreise[24] nach China.

device:

Während diese Varianten der Grand Tour vorwiegend der Selbstoptimierung[25] dienen, hat das freiwillige soziale Jahre auch den Impuls des Helfenswollens, der Solidarität mit den Armen und Notleidenden dieser Welt. Ich kenne junge Erwachsene, die sich um Waisenkinder in Tansania kümmern, um Schwerbehinderte im Libanon und um Flüchtlinge auf Sizilien.

Sogar der Staat engagiert sich, wenn das Gap Year mit sozialer Arbeit kombiniert wird. Der Freiwilligendienst „weltwärts" wird zum Beispiel vom Bundesministerium für Entwicklung[26] finanziert. Seit Gründung im Jahr 2008 sind bald 40000 Freiwillige ausgeschwärmt[27], um anderen und natürlich auch sich selbst bei der Entwicklung zu helfen.

reference:

Manche zweifeln, spotten, das sei doch nichts weiter als ein „Egotrip ins Elend". Gut ausgebildete Helfer könnten viel mehr ausrichten als Leute, die frisch von der Schule kommen. Aber eine großangelegte[28] Evaluierung von „weltwärts" zeigt, dass die Abiturienten durchaus Sinnvolles leisten können und viele wertvolle Einsichten[29] in ihre Heimatländer zurücktragen. Deshalb will die Organisation ihre Zielgruppe erweitern und auch Jugendliche ansprechen, die kein Abitur und keine Akademiker-Eltern haben. […]

[14] doomed – [15] paralysing – [16] undergraduate studies – [17] demands – [18] influence – [19] educational journey – [20] upper middle class – [21] (*fml.*) pupil – [22] finishing touch – [23] to afford sth. – [24] backpacking – [25] self-optimization – [26] Federal Ministry for Economic Cooperation and Development – [27] to swarm out – [28] large-scale – [29] insight; understanding

Die Generation Gap ist eine behütete[30] und ja, vielleicht auch etwas verwöhnte[31] Generation. Sie hat ein sehr freundschaftliches Verhältnis zu ihren Eltern, darf seit frühster Kindheit mitdiskutieren und ist es gewohnt, in allen privaten und politischen Angelegenheiten gefragt zu werden. Sie hat eine beeindruckende Selbständigkeit des Denkens und Meinens ausgebildet, ist aber eher hilflos im praktischen Handeln.

Selten haben sie Weisungen[32] empfangen, selten zu Hause mitgeholfen. Eigentlich fanden sie nichts dabei, sich von ihren Eltern bis ins späte Teenie-Alter bedienen zu lassen. Zugleich ahnen sie, dass es eine große Befreiung sein könnte, selbst einmal zu dienen, sich im Dienst einer größeren Gemeinschaft als nützlich und kompetent zu erleben. Denn im Gefolge[33] von G8 kam nicht nur eine Verkürzung, sondern auch eine Verflachung[34] von Schule. Die sorgt dafür, dass unsere Kinder es nach dem Abi erst einmal gründlich satt haben, Fertig-Wissen[35] in sich hineinzustopfen[36]. Sie hungern danach, als ganze Menschen gefordert[37] zu sein. Nichts wünschen sie sich sehnlicher, als sich einmal durchschlagen[38] zu dürfen in irgendeinem entlegenen[39] Winkel dieser Erde, wo die Tentakeln[40] der elterlichen Zuwendung sie nicht erreichen.

Lassen wir sie ziehen!

https://www.berliner-zeitung.de/lernen-arbeiten/die-generation-gap-auszeit-nach-dem-abitur-li.6062, 6 February 2020 [03.04.2021]

device:

____

____

generation gap:

____

____

____

____

____

____

COMPREHENSION

Scenario:

As a consequence of the Corona pandemic of 2020 and following, many international exchanges and volunteering activities had to be postponed or even cancelled. Now, many people are unsure about what to do. You are a participant of an international youth congress and want to encourage and motivate people and organisations to enable young people to experience volunteering and gap years again.

a) Mediate the German newspaper article and prepare a 5-minute motivational speech on the benefits of gap years.

b) Additionally, point out why – particularly in the aftermath of the Corona pandemic – it is important for young people to get out into the world again.

Tip: Although you are given quite a number of annotations, be careful not to translate the newspaper article word for word. Instead, use the annotations to get a general idea of how to mediate and contextualize the article with regard to the content and its background.

Step 1:

Read the article and highlight or underline relevant key words and phrases with regard to the following topics:

- facts and numbers
- the "Grand Tour" of the past
- gap year and social work
- young people's fears and ambitions
- travelling for everybody
- benefits of gap years and plans for the future

Step 2:

Now sort your findings and mediate them into English. Fill the respective words, phrases and expressions in the grid on page 88.

[30] sheltered – [31] spoiled – [32] orders – [33] aftermath of sth. – [34] banalization – [35] prefabricated knowledge – [36] to stuff sth. into sb./sth. – [37] challenged – [38] to battle one's way – [39] distant – [40] tentacle

facts and numbers	fears and ambitions
• *40,000 volunteers since 2008 (weltwärts)* • • • •	• • • • •
the Grand Tour of the past	**travelling for everybody**
• • • • •	• • • • •
gap year and social work	**benefits/plans for the future**
• • • • •	• • • • •

Tip: You can use the annotations and your dictionary for specific terms – but try to formulate and paraphrase difficult expressions and passages in your own words as much as possible. The Info box below gives you additional help.

Step 3:
Subdivide the article into thematic units and find a suitable headline for each paragraph, using your own words. Take notes in the margin of the page.

Tip: Finally, combine the information you have collected in the previous tasks and prepare your speech.

Step 4:
Think about a concise (*prägnant*) introductory sentence or question to your speech to attract the audience's attention.

Info

Paraphrasing means rewriting somebody else's thoughts or formulations in your own words. This often requires you to
use simpler language and less complex sentences and formulations,
transform technical terms into everyday language convey a message to non-experts,
use synonyms of certain ideas or concepts,
refer to examples to illustrate a complicated or complex matter.

Step 5:
Select the most relevant information from your notes and sort them into the order and structure you want to have for your speech.

Step 6:
Conclude your speech by thanking the audience for their attention and formulate a motivational and appealing final sentence.

Example:
- *Let us all try to overcome the paralyzing emotions of the last years and get active for a bright future.*
- *Let's look forward to making wonderful experiences again …*

A week before ...

- **Set reasonable and realistic periods** to study in.
- Set your study in **chunks of 30 – 60 minutes**, taking a break in-between.

The night before ...

- **Assemble all the tools** you are allowed/required to use during the exam (e. g. paper, pencil, highlighters in different colours, etc.)
- **Get enough sleep:** If you are very nervous, take an outdoor walk or watch a nice movie.
- Eat well and don't forget to take food and something to drink with you to your examination.

Exam day ...

- **Avoid studying immediately before the exam** because this might stress you out. Try to relax.
- **Read** the questions/assignments **thoroughly**; at least two times.
- Pay attention to and **highlight/underline** the **task markers** (*Operatoren*) and **relevant key words** to make sure you have understood exactly what to do and what to focus on.
- Spend some minutes on **planning what you want to write**. Take notes, e. g. draw a mind map or create a linear outline or flowchart which is like a skeleton for what will become your composition.
- Remember to write your composition in **organized paragraphs**. Use one paragraph for one topic. Your paragraphs should be of about 5 – 8 sentences each.
- **Time yourself** right by setting yourself realistic goals for each assignment of the examination. Make sure you can glance at a watch/clock easily to remain on track.
- Try to **finish writing about 20 minutes earlier**.
  - Proof-read your composition, paying attention to spelling and (missing) punctuation.
  - Check your grammar (e.g. irregular verbs, sentence order (S – P – O), etc.).
- Done! ☺

Practise ... Analysing a Non-Fictional Text and Mediating a Magazine Article

Part A: Reading/Writing

Patrick Butler

"Boomerang" Trend of Young Adults Living with Parents Is Rising

High rents, job insecurity and coronavirus are among the reasons cited for nearly two-thirds of under-35s having returned to or remained in the family home.

The so-called "boomerang" phenomenon – young adults returning to their parents' home until well into their 20s or early 30s – is now a permanent feature of UK society and likely to trigger[1] a profound rethink of how many families live their lives, experts have said.

Research found nearly two-thirds of childless single adults aged 20-34 in the UK have either never left or have moved back into the family home because of a combination of a precarious[2] job market and low wages, sky-high private sector rents and life shocks such as relationship breakups.

Around 3.5 million single young adults in the UK are estimated to live with their parents, an increase of a third over the past decade, and a trend that is likely to accelerate as the economic and social impact of the coronavirus pandemic deepens.

"Children living at home well into their 20s is not a temporary phenomenon, it's here to stay," said Katherine Hill, senior research associate at the Centre for Research in Social Policy at Loughborough University. "A lot of young people will spend most of a decade of their lives living like this."

Staying on in the family home when childhood ends is now common across all ethnic backgrounds and most income groups as opportunities for young adults to fly the nest[3] diminish[4].

The Loughborough research – the first large-scale quantitative study into the phenomenon – found 71% of young single adults were living with their parents during their early 20s, and a majority (54%) were living at the parental home in their late 20s, falling to a third of those in their early 30s.

The prospect[5] of sharing a home for up to 10 years after children grow up – though they may dip in and out[6] as life circumstances dictate – may require a significant recalibration[7] of expectations for parents and children, and possibly a reassessment[8] of life plans on both sides, researchers said.

Families must negotiate[9] over issues such as whether the twenty-something sons and daughters pay rent, contribute to bills and help with household chores[10]. Issues of privacy and independence arise, especially if the home is overcrowded. These sorts of conversations, researchers noted, "can cause some anguish[11]".

[1] **to trigger** to cause sth. to start – [2] **precarious** full of a lack of security or stability – [3] **to fly the nest** to leave home – [4] **to diminish** to reduce – [5] **prospect** the possibility that sth. might happen in the future – [6] **to dip in and out** to do sth. only briefly and start sth. new – [7] **recalibration** the act of changing sth. to fit a new situation – [8] **reassessment** the act of changing your view of the importance or value of sth. – [9] **to negotiate** *verhandeln* – [10] **chore** [tʃɔːr] a job that is often boring or unpleasant but needs to be done regularly – [11] **anguish** extreme unhappiness

Coronavirus disruption[12] is believed to have encouraged the trend, with university closures, the shift to remote working, job losses and furloughs[13] increasing the likelihood of adult children returning to the parental home in recent months – or, alternatively, forcing them to abandon plans to leave it.

"For my generation living at your parents' home in your 20s is not something shameful or abnormal," said Tabitha-Levis Jarsdel, 24, a graduate who lives with her mother near Portsmouth. '"No one is shocked when you meet people [your own age] and you say, 'I live at home'. Most of the time they say, 'me too'."

Jarsdel moved home after graduating in 2019 to work for a year and save up enough to move to London to take up a postgraduate[14] course. The volatile[15] jobs market meant she has had to put off[16] those plans for another year. "Most of my friends still live at home or are planning to move back when they finish university."

While losing the independence she enjoyed at university was a shock, Jarsdel says she is lucky that her mum is supportive and they get on well. Older generations can be patronising, she said, often implying that living at home is a sign of failure. "There's going to have to be some sort of change because everyone is affected."

The research, funded by the Standard Life Foundation, estimated a young adult moving back in with parents might typically save £120 a week in rent, fuel and council tax[17] bills compared with living in a one-bedroom flat. Depending on the level of offspring contribution[18], parents on the other hand may find they are worse off.

Low-income households are more likely to see living standards fall if adult children live at home because the benefit system would reduce their payments. A family on benefits with a 24-year-old at home is typically £90 a week worse off, relative to its basic living costs, compared with having a child aged 14, the research suggested.

The growing cost of housing has fuelled[19] the boomerang trend, with the proportion of adults aged 25 – 34 owning a home falling from 55 % in 1996 to 34 % in 2016. Renting privately consumed 9 % of tenants'[20] income on average in 1961; by 2017 it accounted for 36 %. Stagnating[21] wages and insecure employment for young people are also factors.

https://www.theguardian.com/society/2020/oct/18/boomerang-trend-of-young-adults-living-with-parents-is-rising-study, 18 October 2020 [04.04.2021]

ASSIGNMENTS

Part A: Reading/Writing

1. Give an outline of the (recent) trend of young adults returning to their parents' home as well as its causes and consequences for the families.
   (Comprehension)

2. Examine the author's stance on the "Boomerang" trend by analysing the structure of the article and the examples given and referred to in the text.
   (Analysis)

[12] **disruption** *Diskontinuität* – [13] **furlough** *Beurlaubung* – [14] **postgraduate** a student who has already received a university degree and studies further for a more advanced degree – [15] **volatile** likely to change suddenly and unexpectedly, usually by getting worse – [16] **to put sth. off** (*phr. v.*) to delay sth. until a later time – [17] **council tax** *Kommunalsteuer* – [18] **offspring contribution** money that the children pay to the family budget – [19] **to fuel** to increase sth. or make sth. stronger – [20] **tenant** a person who pays rent to land, house or flat – [21] **to stagnate** to stay the same and not grow or develop

3. You have a choice here. Choose one of the following tasks.

   3.1 "Most of my friends still live at home or are planning to move back when they finish university." (ll. 53 ff.) Comment on Tabitha-Levis Jarsdell's statements and state whether (or not) you share her view that it is "normal" that 24-year-old graduates like her still live with their parents and "give up their independence". (*Comment/Evaluation*)

   3.2 You are a frustrated parent who thinks that young adults should leave their parents' home after graduating and start a life of their own.
   Against the background of the information given in the article, write a letter to your local politician or constituency candidate (*Wahlkreiskandidat*) in which you describe the intolerable situation and demand political, social and economic changes (e. g. cheaper housing, better paid jobs for post-graduates, etc.). ((*Re-*)*Creation of text*)

Part B: Mediation

Schlimmer als Helikopter-Eltern[1]? – Achtung, Rasenmäher-Eltern[2]

Immer häufiger greifen[3] Eltern in das Spiel oder die sozialen Begegnungen[4] ihrer Kinder ein. Sie entfernen potentielle Hindernisse[5], bevor ihr Kind darüber stolpern[6] könnte, sie ebnen den Weg. Diese neue Generation von Eltern bezeichnen Experten als "Rasenmäher-Eltern". [...]

Rasenmäher-Eltern machen ihren Kindern den Weg frei

"Rasenmäher-Eltern tun alles, was nötig ist, um ihr Kind vor Rückschlägen[7], Auseinandersetzungen[8] oder Misserfolgen zu bewahren. Anstatt ihre Kinder auf Herausforderungen vorzubereiten, mähen sie Hindernisse nieder, sodass ihre Kinder sie gar nicht erst zu spüren bekommen."

Das klingt vielleicht erstmal recht harmlos. Doch der Lehrer erklärt weiter:

"Indem wir Kinder großziehen, die nur wenige Auseinandersetzungen erlebt haben, erschaffen wir keine glücklichere Generation von Kindern. Wir erschaffen eine Generation, die keine Ahnung hat, was sie tun soll, wenn sie tatsächlich mal auf ein Hindernis stößt. Eine Generation, die beim bloßen Gedanken an einen Misserfolg in Panik ausbricht oder komplett abschaltet. Eine Generation, für die Scheitern so schmerzhaft ist, dass sie Bewältigungsmechanismen wie Sucht, Schuldzuweisung[9] und Verinnerlichung[10] benötigt, um damit klarzukommen."

Auch eine Professorin einer amerikanischen Universität in Pittsburgh berichtet in einem Blogbeitrag anonym über ihre Erfahrungen mit Rasenmäher-Eltern – und beschreibt die gravierenden Folgen des Erziehungsstils für die Kinder:

Sie entwickeln keine eigene Motivation und haben keinen eigenen Antrieb, denn sie wissen nur, wie man dem Weg folgt, den die Rasenmäher-Eltern bereits vorbereitet haben.

Sie sind nicht in der Lage, große oder kleine Entscheidungen zu treffen, ohne Hilfestellung von anderen.

Sie bekommen ständig die Botschaft vermittelt, dass sie nicht gut genug sind, um ihre eigenen Probleme zu lösen. [...]

Erfolgreiche Kinder um jeden Preis

Nicht nur in den USA, auch in Deutschland sehen Experten die Gefahren eines solchen Erziehungsstils[11] für die Kinder. Immer häufiger wird auch hierzulande darüber berichtet, dass Kinder Aufgaben abbrechen, hinschmeißen, zornig, oder trotzig[12] reagieren, wenn sie auf eine Herausforderung stoßen. Die Angst vor dem Scheitern ist so groß, dass manche Kinder sich gar nicht erst an eine Aufgabe herantrauen.

"Wenn Kinder nie lernen, Enttäuschungen oder Rückschläge hinnehmen zu müssen, werden sie zu schwachen Persönlichkeiten ", warnte der Sozial-, Bildungs- und Gesundheitsforscher Klaus Hurrelmann. Kein Kind könne lebenstüchtig[13] werden, wenn man ihm nie gestatte, auch mal ein Risiko einzugehen. Es sei wichtig, auch die Erfahrung zu machen, dass Hindernisse überwunden werden können.

[1] helicopter parents; overprotective parents – [2] lawnmower parents – [3] to interfere with sth. – [4] encounter– [5] obstacle – [6] to stumble – [7] setback – [8] controversy, argument – [9] accusation – [10] internalization – [11] educational style – [12] stubborn – [13] able to cope with life

Doch Kinder von "Rasenmäher-Eltern" stoßen kaum einmal auf ein Hindernis. Sie sind es gewohnt, einem vorgegebenen Weg zu folgen. Ihre Eltern wollen sie – vermutlich aus falsch verstandener Liebe – vor negativen Erfahrungen bewahren.

Gleichzeitig haben sie eine sehr hohe Erwartungshaltung[14] an ihre Kinder. Sie greifen auch deshalb so stark in ihr Leben ein, weil sie wollen, dass die Kinder sie sie erfolgreich sehen wollen – ob nun in sozialer oder akademischer Hinsicht. [...]

Die gut gemeinte Hilfestellung der Eltern wird dann schnell zum Problem. Durch das ständige Üben mit dem Kind haben die Eltern sich stark eingemischt[15]. Vielen ist nicht bewusst, dass dieses Verhalten ein Kind stark unter Druck setzt und ihm das Gefühl vermittelt, dass die Eltern etwas Besseres von ihm erwarten. [...]

Eltern haben mehr Angst als Generationen vor ihnen

Gleichzeitig muss man sich aber auch fragen, wo die Ursache für das eigene Verhalten liegt. Warum fällt es Eltern zunehmend schwer, auf die Kompetenz ihrer Kinder zu vertrauen? Warum haben immer mehr Eltern das Gefühl, die Kontrolle übernehmen zu müssen – etwa, indem sie gemeinsam mit den Kindern Hausaufgaben machen?

Eine Erklärung lautet, dass Eltern heute mehr Angst haben, als die Generationen vor ihnen. Angst vor Gefahren. Angst vor dem Scheitern. Angst vor Ausgrenzung[16]. Vielleicht haben sie selbst schlechte Erfahrungen in der Schule gemacht. Vielleicht wollen sie einfach nur, dass es ihren Kindern in jeder Hinsicht besser ergeht als ihnen selbst.

Wer Kinder hat, kennt diese Angst bestimmt und kann sie nachvollziehen. Doch diese Angst muss überwunden[17] werden. Damit sie unsere Kinder nicht belastet[18] und davon abhält, zu den großartigen Persönlichkeiten heranzuwachsen, die sie sind – ganz ohne unsere Hilfe.

Vielleicht ist das die schwierigste und zugleich die wichtigste Aufgabe, die Eltern haben.

https://www.focus.de/familie/eltern/familie-heute/familie-rasenmaeher-eltern-experten-warnen-vor-den-folgen-des-neuen-erziehungsstils_id_9663538.html, © https://www.weareteachers.com/lawnmower-parents, 30 August 2018 [03.04.2021]

ASSIGNMENTS

Part B: Mediation

Your American e-twinning partner Alex is doing a project on "over-protective parents" in his social sciences class and has asked you whether this is a common phenomenon in Germany as well.

You have come across the article published in the German weekly magazine *Focus*. Write an e-mail to Alex in which you outline the aspects and new trends depicted in the article and inform him about

a) possible causes and
b) the reported consequences that result in the critical situation.

[14] expectations – [15] to interfere with sth. – [16] exclusion – [17] to overcome sth. – [18] to strain, to burden

Practise ... Analysing a Fictional Text and Mediating a Magazine Article

Part A: Reading/Writing

Marieke Lucas Rijneveld

The Discomfort of Evening

Ten-year-old Jas, the protagonist of the novel, lives with her family on a farm in the Netherlands. With Christmas approaching, Jas is scared that her father might kill her beloved rabbit Dieuwertje for the Christmas Eve dinner. In the scene at hand, Jas is angry because she was denied going ice-skating with her brother Matthies. The scene following the excerpt describes that her younger brother Matthies had broken into the ice and died.

"Once he's got his mind set on something, there's no budging[1] him," my granny on the most religious side of the family sometimes said and that was why I suspected he was feeding up my rabbit Dieuwertje, which I'd got from Lien next door, for the big Christmas dinner in two days' time. [...] He'd once said that the neck vertebrae[2] were the most breakable part of a body – I heard them snapping in my head as though my mother was breaking a handful of raw vermicelli[3] above the pan – and a rope with a noose[4] in had recently appeared in the attic, hanging from the rafters[5]. "It's for a swing," Dad said, but there was still no swing. I didn't understand why the rope was hanging in the attic and not in the shed with the screwdrivers and his collection of bolts[6]. [...] I briefly pictured my rabbit hanging broken-necked from the rope in the attic, behind Matthies's bed, so that our father could skin it more easily. It would probably come off the same way as the skin from the big cooked sausage that Mum peeled with her potato knife in the morning: only they'd put Dieuwertje in a layer of butter in the big casserole dish on the gas stove, and the whole house would smell of broiled rabbit. [...] I'd noticed that while I used to be sparing[7] with the feed, I was now allowed to give my rabbit a whole scoopful[8], as well as the carrot tops. Despite the fact that he was a buck[9], I'd named him after the curly-haired female presenter on children's TV because I found her so pretty. [...] I pictured the way Dad would use that hand to wring my rabbit's neck, like the child-proof top of a canister of nitrogen[10]: here was only one right way to do it. I imagined Mum laying out my lifeless pet on the silver dish she used for Russian salad on Sundays after church. She'd display him on a bed of lamb's lettuce[11] and garnish him with gherkins, tomato chunks, grated carrot and a sprig[12] of thyme. [...]

I pressed my forehead harder and harder against the edge of my bed; I felt the pressure of cold wood on my skin and closed my eyes. Sometimes I found it strange that you had you had to pray in the dark, although maybe it was like my glow-in-the-dark duvet[13]: the stars and the planets only emitted light and protected you from the night when it was dark enough. God must work in the same way.

[1] **budging** moving – [2] **neck vertebrae** *Rückenwirbel* – [3] **vermicelli** *Fadennudeln* – [4] **noose** *Schlinge* – [5] **rafter** any large piece of wood that supports a roof; *Dachsparren* – [6] **bolt** a metal bar on a door or window that slides across to lock it closed – [7] **to spare** (*archaic*) to save sth.; *sparen* – [8] **a scoopful** *eine Schaufel (voll)* – [9] **buck** a male animal (here: rabbit) – [10] **nitrogen** ['naɪtrədʒən] *Stickstoff* – [11] **lamb's lettuce** *Feldsalat* – [12] **sprig** a single small plant stem with leaves on it – [13] **duvet** *Federbett*

I let my intertwined[14] hands rest on my knees. Angrily I thought about Matthies who'd be drinking hot chocolate from one of the stalls on the ice. I thought of him skating with red cheeks, and about the thaw[15] that would start tomorrow: the curly-haired presenter had warned of roofs that might be too slippery for Saint Nicholas to get down the chimney, and mist[16] which might lead him to get lost and perhaps Matthies too, even though it was his own fault. For a moment, I saw my skates before me, greased and back in their box, ready to be returned to the attic.

I thought about being too small for so much, but that no one told you when you are being big enough, how many centimetres on the door-post[17] was, and I asked God if He please couldn't take my brother Matthies instead of my rabbit. "Amen".

from *The Discomfort of Evening* by Marieke Lucas Rijneveld. Faber & Faber, London 2020, pp. 12 ff.

ASSIGNMENTS

Part A: Reading/Writing

1. Present Jas's desperate situation, its causes and Jas's way of finding a solution.
   (*Comprehension*)

2. Explain the narrator's way of describing her hopeless situation and fears.
   Which narrative and stylistic devices are employed to turn on the reader's "inner cinema" (*Kopfkino*) and imagination?
   (*Analysis*)

3. You have a choice here. Choose **one** of the following tasks.

   3.1 "I thought about being too small for so much ..." (l. 45).
   Reflect on Jas's fears and concerns expressed in the excerpt and state whether (or not) you consider them to be understandable or whether Jas is just being hysterical and overreacting.
   (*Comment/Evaluation*)

   3.2 Considering the various hints and clues given in the excerpt (e. g. the swing, Christmas dinner, Matthies's death), imagine Christmas Eve has finally come.
   Write another scene and describe what might happen next.
   ((*Re-*)*Creation of text*)

[14] **to intertwine** to twist; *verschränken* – [15] **thaw** a period of warmer weather when snow and ice begin to melt – [16] **mist** *Dunst* – [17] **centimetres on the door-post** scratches made on the door-post in order to see how much children have grown

Part B: Mediation

Ute Eberle, Susanne Gilges

Geschwister: Von der Liebe unter Rivalen

Die Beziehungen unter Schwestern und Brüdern sind urwüchsiger[1] und spontaner als alle anderen menschlichen Bindungen. Zu Rivalitäten kommt es schon im Mutterleib[2].

Rund zwei Drittel aller Kinder in Deutschland wissen das aus eigener Erfahrung: Sie wachsen mit Schwestern und Brüdern auf. Die Bindung zwischen ihnen hält meist länger als jede andere in ihrem Leben. Eltern sterben, Freundschaften vergehen, Partnerschaften enden im Streit – aber Geschwister[3] bleiben.

Sie sind dabei, wenn wir das erste Mal vom Ein-Meter-Brett[4] springen. Sie spielen mit uns Fangen[5] im Garten. Sie helfen, die Scherben[6] der Vase zu verstecken – und verraten der Mutter dann doch, wer sie zerbrochen hat.

Sie sind unsere ersten Gefährten als Babys, unsere Vertrauten[7] als Kinder, unsere Folterknechte[8] in den Teenagerjahren, wenn sie uns zur Weißglut[9] reizen mit einer sorgfältig platzierten Anspielung auf die verpatzte Mathearbeit. Als junge Erwachsene ignorieren wir sie oft, das eigene Leben ist dann wichtiger. Doch im Alter kommen sie uns häufig wieder nah. Wir lehnen uns an sie, wenn Partner sterben oder uns Krankheiten schwächen.

Geschwisterbeziehungen sind urwüchsiger und spontaner als jede andere Beziehung, so der Münchner Psychologe Hartmut Kasten. Die Liebe zwischen Brüdern und Schwestern kann bis zum Inzest[10] reichen, der Hass bis zum Mord. Es ist ein ganz eigenes Kraftfeld[11], eine eigene Psychodynamik, die zwischen Geschwistern herrscht.

Doch erst seit etwa 20 Jahren beschäftigen sich Wissenschaftler ernsthaft mit dem Verhältnis unter Brüdern und Schwestern. Dabei haben Psychologen, Soziologen und Genetiker[12] festgestellt: Für unser Selbstbild und unsere Identität ist die Beziehung zu unseren Geschwistern in vielerlei Hinsicht ebenso prägend[13] wie die zu unseren Eltern – ja manchmal sogar prägender.

Denn Geschwister bilden die erste soziale Gruppe, in die wir uns einfügen müssen. In der wir lernen, mit den Nuancen von Nähe, Ablehnung[14], Konkurrenz, Konflikt und Versöhnung[15] umzugehen.

„Der Schatz an Gefühlen, Denkmustern[16] und Handlungsstrategien, den wir mit Geschwistern entwickeln, wird zum Grundmuster[17] für den Umgang mit der Welt", schreibt der Schweizer Psychologe Jürg Frick.

Bereits Einjährige haben mit ihren Geschwistern ebenso viel Umgang und Austausch wie mit ihren Müttern. Im Alter zwischen drei und fünf Jahren verbringen Brüder und Schwestern häufig sogar mehr als doppelt so viel Zeit miteinander wie mit den Eltern.

Dabei sind Geschwister – biologisch gesehen – vor allem eines: Rivalen. [...]

[1] unspoiled – [2] womb – [3] siblings – [4] 1 meter springboard – [5] chase – [6] shards – [7] confidant – [8] torturer – [9] rage – [10] incest – [11] field of force – [12] geneticist – [13] formative – [14] refusal, rejection – [15] reconciliation – [16] thought pattern – [17] basic pattern

Vermutlich findet auch im menschlichen Mutterleib eine Art Verdrängungskampf[18] statt. Immerhin kommt bei eineiigen Zwillingen[19] meist das eine Kind kleiner und schwächer zur Welt als das andere. Später konkurrieren Geschwister vor allem um die elterliche Zuneigung[20] und Fürsorge[21] – auch das begrenzte Ressourcen, die nicht unbedingt gleich verteilt sind. Die meisten Eltern mögen zwar behaupten, dass sie jeden Sprössling gleich behandeln. Doch fest steht: Sie tun es nicht. [...]

Mit jedem Sprössling fällt der Umgang anders aus. So sagen die meisten Geschwisterkinder, ihre Mütter seien parteiisch[22]. Und viele Eltern geben zu, insgeheim Favoriten zu haben. Doch auch die fairsten Väter und Mütter könnten ihre Kinder nicht genau gleich erziehen: Sie sind aufgeregt und unsicher beim ersten, zunehmend routiniert bei jedem weiteren Kind. Allein eine Krankheit oder das Alter des Kindes erfordern unterschiedliches Handeln. Und selbst wenn Eltern die gleichen Regeln anwenden, prägen diese jedes Kind anders.

So fühlen sich viele ältere Geschwister vernachlässigt[23], wenn sich die Eltern um das Neugeborene kümmern. Obwohl sie als Babys die gleiche Fürsorge genossen haben, nehmen sie das Verhalten der Eltern nun aus einem anderen Blickwinkel wahr – und sind voller Neid[24]. [...]

Auch wenn Zank im Kinderzimmer normal ist und Rivalität ein gesunder Entwicklungsmotor[25] sein kann – manche Hänselei[26] verfolgt uns ein Leben lang. Fühlen wir uns etwa in der Firma stets gering geschätzt[27], kann das daran liegen, dass eine unaufgearbeitete[28] Geschwisterbeziehung unsere Wahrnehmung verzerrt[29]. [...]

Weitgehend unerforscht ist, wie sich das Zerbrechen und Neu-Verflechten von Familienbanden auf Geschwister auswirkt. Demnächst wird wohl mehr als jedes sechste Kind in Deutschland die Scheidung der Eltern erleben. Und etwa eine Million Kinder leben in „Patchworkfamilien", die entstehen, wenn Elternteile mit einem neuen Partner zusammenleben. Dann bilden sich oft Kombinationen aus Stief[30]- und Halbgeschwistern[31]. Noch mehr Jugendliche wachsen ohne Geschwister auf: Drei von zehn Kindern sind Einzelkinder, in Großstädten beträgt ihr Anteil sogar bis zu 50 Prozent. Doch entgegen ihrem früheren Ruf[32] handelt es sich dabei keinesfalls nur um verhätschelte[33] und sozial verkümmerte[34] Egozentriker. Vielmehr zeigen Studien, dass Einzelkinder besonders selbstständig und wohl ebenso sozial kompetent sind wie Geschwisterkinder, dazu oft ein hohes Selbstbewusstsein haben.

Denn natürlich ist ein Leben ohne Geschwister in vielem einfacher: keinc abgelegten[35] Kleider. Kein kleiner Bruder, der einem nachspioniert. Kein Zoff um die Spielkonsole. Keine quälende Hassliebe[36]. Keiner, der lachend Peinlichkeiten[37] aus den Kindertagen zum Besten gibt.

Aber auch keiner, der herbeieilt, um einen auf dem Schulhof vor Mitschülern zu schützen.

https://www.geo.de/magazine/geo-kompakt/6774-rtkl-kindheit-geschwister-von-der-liebe-unter-rivalen, GEO KOMPAKT Nr. 17 – 12/08 [05.04.2021]

[18] fight for survival – [19] identical twins – [20] affection – [21] care – [22] biased, partial – [23] neglected – [24] envy – [25] power for development – [26] teasing – [27] underestimated – [28] unresolved – [29] distorted – [30] stepsiblings – [31] half siblings – [32] reputation – [33] pampered – [34] stunted – [35] discarded – [36] love-hate relationship – [37] embarrassments

ASSIGNMENTS

Part B: Mediation

Your Australian pen pal Amanda has asked you for help: She has to do coursework on the topic of "sibling rivalry" for her pedagogics class at school and does not know where to begin.
You have found the article at hand, published in the German magazine *Geo*, that perfectly matches your friend's coursework topic. Write an outline of the magazine article in which you present the relevant aspects and e-mail it to your friend Amanda.

Webcodes

All audio and audio-visual material as well as suggestions for solutions are provided on **webcodes**.
In order to use the webcodes, access the website www.westermann.de/webcode and enter the respective code or scan the QR codes.

@ WES-121502-001
@ WES-121502-002
@ WES-121502-003
@ WES-121502-004
@ WES-121502-005
@ WES-121502-006
@ WES-121502-007
@ WES-121502-008
@ WES-121502-009
@ WES-121502-010
@ WES-121502-011
@ WES-121502-012
@ WES-121502-013
@ WES-121502-014
@ WES-121502-015
@ WES-121502-016
@ WES-121502-017

Acknowledgements

Images

|Alamy Stock Photo, Abingdon/Oxfordshire: dedMazay 58.1; PHOTOlink 7.1. |Baaske Cartoons, Müllheim: Plaßmann, Thomas 51.1. |CartoonStock.com, Bath: 6.1, 12.1, 18.1, 30.1, 76.1, 84.1, 89.1; Judd, Phil 70.1; Nixon, Roy 80.1; Ritchie, Scot 50.1; Wildt, Chris 54.1. |Deutsche Welle, Bonn: 39.1, 39.2, 39.3. |Guardian News & Media Limited, London: Jefferson, Manny 61.1. |Herrera Carcedo, Diego, Burgos: 77.1. |iStockphoto.com, Calgary: appleuzr 35.1; Le_Mon 35.3; Novruzova, Turac 34.1; RaulAlmu 35.4; undrey 35.2; zager 36.1. |Market Business News: 55.1. |Shutterstock.com, New York: Benge, Alan 42.1; Purcell, Don 63.1. |stock.adobe.com, Dublin: Jemastock 15.1; kilroy79 15.2. |toonpool.com, Berlin, Castrop-Rauxel: Tomaschoff, Jan 24.1; Zach 52.1. |UNICEF Deutschland, Köln: © UNICEF/UN0509257/Nkosilathi Nyathi 43.1. |United Nations: https://www.un.org/sustainabledevelopment/ "The content of this publication has not been approved by the United Nations and does not reflect the views of the United Nations or its officials or Member States" 49.1.